LANDSCAPE
REJUVENATION

LANDSCAPE REJUVENATION

REMODELING THE HOME LANDSCAPE

Bonnie Lee Appleton, Ph.D.

Photographs by the author
Illustrations by Cynthia Locklin

A Garden Way Publishing Book

Storey Communications, Inc.
Pownal, Vermont 05261

The information in this book is true and complete to the best of our knowledge. All recommendations are made without guarantee on the part of the author or Storey Communications, Inc. The author and publisher disclaim all liability incurred with the use of this information.

Text design by Wanda Harper
Production by Wanda Harper
Cover design by Wanda Harper
Cover photograph by Bill Pinkham,
  Landscape Architect
Back cover drawing by Cynthia Locklin
Back cover photo by the author
Color slides converted to black and white by Michael
  Griffin, Cambridge, New York
Typesetting by Hemmings Motor News, Bennington,
  Vermont

The editor would like to acknowledge the help of Bernie Graney, Dale Moore, and Mary Pat Glover in converting the author's electronic manuscript to type.

Printed in the United States by W. A. Krueger Company
First printing May 1988

Library of Congress Cataloging-in-Publication Data
Appleton, Bonnie Lee, 1948-
  Landscape rejuvenation.

  Includes index.
  1. Landscape gardening.   I. Title.
SB473.A66   1988   712'.6   87-42970
ISBN 0-88266-495-6
ISBN 0-88266-496-4 (pbk.)

To family and friends
who have been so
tolerant and supportive

CONTENTS

Preface

A very comprehensive and commendable booklet was published by the Weyerhaeuser Company in celebration of their tenth year of involvement in the nursery industry. Titled *The Value of Landscaping,* it takes both a qualitative and a quantitative look at home landscaping, and indicates that the renovation or relandscaping of homes holds great potential for the nursery industry.

To that end this book was written. There are many books on landscape design available, but very few deal with the subject of home landscape renovation in detail. And yet how many people come home each night to a landscape with overgrown shrubs, bare lawn areas, or a desire for more functional space around them?

So many landscape design books are filled with lists of plants to use, and for that reason this book lacks such suggestions. For any locale there are many good sources of plant lists (a retail garden center or the extension service in your area are your best bets), and too often the lists in design books tend to regionalize the book.

What I have tried to do is to take a more analytical look at landscape renovation, centering as much on why it is needed as on how to do it. If you understand why a landscape has come to need renovation, I feel you will be better able to design a "new" landscape and to maintain that new landscape in such a way that future renovations will be minimized.

You will see very average examples of landscape scenes and plants pictured in this book. Too many design books tend to glorify the best of everything and don't "show it like it is" in the real world. The examples come from many places: from Stillwater, Oklahoma, and Long Beach Island, New Jersey, to Louisville, Kentucky, and Virginia Beach, Virginia. They include examples not just of the plants and landscapes of total strangers, but of landscapes that have been my own.

Though I taught landscape design for several years at a community college in St. Louis, it was not until I started giving talks on landscape renovation as an extension specialist, first in Kentucky and then in Virginia, that the idea of doing a book began to form. And it was only with encouragement from a student in a Master Gardener class that I really took the idea to heart.

With the increased realization and appreciation by realtors and the general public of the value that a good landscape can add to a house, more and more old landscapes are getting a face-lift, both by professional nurserymen, landscape architects and designers, and by homeowners.

It is my hope that if you are about to undertake a landscape renovation project you will find the information and illustrations in this book to be helpful and useful.

Bonnie Lee Appleton
Virginia Beach, Virginia
March 1987

LANDSCAPE
REJUVENATION

1

WHY LANDSCAPES MAY NEED RENOVATION

Call it landscape rejuvenation, landscape remodeling, or landscape redesign. Whatever the name, the implication is that something that already exists in the landscape needs redoing. That need to redo, unfortunately, causes many people who decide to undertake this activity to do so with a disgruntled feeling, a feeling that they have done something wrong. Thus the renovation of a home landscape can feel like an unwanted chore. If the various reasons a landscape may need renovation are reviewed, however, you will often see that landscape renovation can be thought of very positively. This difference in attitude can turn what was perceived as a chore into a very enjoyable project.

The inclusive term "landscape renovation" will be used throughout this book because it includes many activities. Plants may need to be moved — relocation. Plants may need to be pruned and nursed back to health — rejuvenation. Planting beds may need to be built again — reconstruction, or their boundaries delineated — redesign. Older forms of plants that are more prone to insect and disease problems may need to be removed and possibly replaced. The list of "redo"-type terms could continue, but what in summary is represented by all of these activities is the renovation of a landscape.

A landscape renovation project should be undertaken with a desire to improve the existing landscape and a willingness to make the necessary changes. There is no point in sparing a favorite plant that has a useful life of no more than another year or two if it will impose a hardship on the renovation process by making the redesign of a bed or the maintenance of surrounding plants difficult. A landscape renovation project can require considerable energy and resources — new plants, permanent features, labor — therefore the project should not be hampered by retaining plants that cannot realistically be rejuvenated or that won't fit smoothly into a new design (Figures 1-1 and 1-2).

WHY A LANDSCAPE RENOVATION MAY BE NECESSARY

The reasons for renovating a landscape can be as varied and numerous as the landscape renovation projects themselves, and they are enumerated below. In most instances several factors contribute to the status of a landscape, and these must be recognized so that the work can be done properly.

1

Figure 1-1. This blue spruce is dying; it should be removed and not imposed on a new design.

Figure 1-2. A dead tree trunk is not a valuable landscape feature, even if used as a planter, but instead only detracts from it and should be completely removed.

At times homeowners are at fault. They may have planted too many plants too close together many years ago in an attempt to create instantly mature landscapes. This overplanting and crowding is generally most evident in the area immediately in front of and adjacent to a house — the area where tradition has dictated that we develop a foundation planting (Figure 1-3). This phenomenon often occurs even with professionally designed landscapes because many designers have little or no experience with landscape maintenance, and frequently don't even have a good idea how large the plants they specify will grow, or at what rate.

Foundation plantings were originally designed to hide the foot or more of exposed foundation that is readily seen above the soil line around the bottom of older-style houses. But residential architecture is constantly undergoing changes, with innovations in residential landscape design lagging far behind. Few houses designed today "need" foundation plantings because raised or exposed foundations are no longer typical design features (Figure 1-4). Despite this we still find most new homes being planted with these now unnecessary coverups, and too frequently faced or fronted with boring straight lines of evergreens instead of skillful massings of plants of varying colors and textures backed up by evergreens. The "foundation" or front area should be designed as an entryway that blends or coordinates with the architectural style of the house as well as with the rest of the landscape.

Many homeowners don't properly care for the plants in their landscape — neglecting to control insects and disease or failing to water during periods of drought. In addition they frequently fail to recognize the importance of such things as feeding not only their turf grasses, but also their landscape plants, both to encourage establishment growth of young plants and to help older plants stay vigorous. The lack of design expertise or forethought becomes very obvious as their landscapes grow.

For many homeowners landscape renovations are necessary because they have purchased an older home whose landscape is aesthetically displeasing to them or had been neglected by the previous owner. Renovation of a landscape should even be considered before a house is put up for sale in order to increase its appeal and monetary value. Unfortunately, a landscape renovation situation

Figure 1-3.   New houses often have "overplanted" land-scapes to make them look immediately mature. In this case, there are too many evergreens planted too close together, all of which will, in a few years, outgrow their limited space around the foundation.

can even occur with a brand-new house in which a quick just-to-get-by design was developed, where a poor planting job was done, or where cheap, common, or poor quality plants were used (Figure 1-5).

In a more positive light, many people should view the need for landscape renovation as an acknowledgment that they have done many things correctly. They did control pest problems, they did water and fertilize when needed. They did a good job of growing the trees, shrubs, and other plants that populate their landscapes, and as a result the plants responded and grew (Figure 1-6). Plants can overgrow a landscape due to either good care or careless neglect.

Landscapes may require renovation for non-plant reasons. As a family grows its needs change and, therefore, its outdoor living environment may also need to change. Natural disasters such as tor-nadoes, floods, storm winds, or hurricanes can damage landscapes to the extent that they need renovation (Figure 1-7). As new technology comes along, such as in-ground irrigation systems, people want to take advantage of these advances. And of-tentimes other changes in the landscape — over-head utility lines being buried, sidewalks and curbs being installed — are beyond the control of the homeowner and may necessitate renovation.

Herein lies one of the clues to renovation think-ing. Plants grow and facilities change, and these

Figure 1-4.   Houses that do not have exposed foundations give the homeowner greater landscape flexibility because there's no need to conceal unsightly concrete footings.

Figure 1-5. To make a new home more attractive to prospective buyers, a "quick" landscape is often installed. Such
a landscape would be overplanted with poor-quality evergreen shrubs, the lawn would be sparse and unattractive,
and occasional specimen trees would be thoughtlessly
placed (above).

Figure 1-6. Sometimes landscapes are too successful
(these plants have been carefully mulched and pruned). A
few of the plants above have grown so well, and large, that
they detract from the whole design.

Figure 1-7. A surprise spring ice-and-snow storm ripped this saucer magnolia, already in bloom, apart.

factors make it necessary for us to make adjustments. We should begin to condition ourselves to the fact that landscapes are not static. Changes occur frequently in a landscape, and it isn't at all unrealistic to think of undertaking a major landscape renovation project every ten to fifteen years as some horticulturists suggest.

When we rearrange the furniture in a room, buy a new chair, or reupholster an old chair, we're not doing it because the furniture grew. Our tastes changed or something began to wear out. The same can happen with regard to a home landscape. Our tastes may change or a plant, with a finite life span, may simply "wear out." In many instances plants were put in when the house was new and the family young. Then as the house got older it may have been added on to, and was undoubtedly painted, sided, or reshingled on the outside. The needs of families, and possibly even of houses themselves, change, and therefore, landscapes will also need to change.

In fact, the available space within, and the exterior condition of a house, should be evaluated, and changes or additions made prior to renovating the landscape. This will insure that the new landscape will coordinate with changes made to the house and will avoid damage to new plants when work is done to the house. In some cases the landscape may actually be harmful or reduce the value of a home (Figure 1-8). Roots growing into the foundation, branches falling on the roof and damaging shingles or tiles, or twigs scratching against the house in the wind and wearing the paint away are good examples of landscape liabilities.

Figure 1-8.   Most homeowners are unaware of the extent to which the growth of a vine, in this case English ivy, can damage and deface a structure when it needs to be removed.

Figure 1-9. A successful landscape renovation should produce a yard and property that will be beautiful, admirable, manageable, and useful.

WHEN TO BEGIN THE RENOVATION PROCESS

For a new house with a bad or inadequate landscape the renovation job can most often start immediately. So too with the landscape of a fairly new house that the occupants have owned for several years and who have experienced all of its seasonal changes.

But when an older house with a landscape in need of renovation is purchased, a slower approach may be advisable so that a full evaluation of the existing plants can be made. If the house is bought in the winter when the deciduous trees and shrubs are without leaves it may be difficult to correctly identify the plants. Something that looks undesirable in the winter may turn out to be a magnificent plant come spring. In addition there may be bulbs and other perennial plants hidden underground that won't make their presence known until the growing season starts. Many of them may be worth keeping, at least to divide and relocate, and therefore time should be allowed to see the whole landscape develop.

Take a systematic approach for a landscape renovation project. Rather than start with a shovel, chain saw, and pruning shears, start with a pencil and ruler. A landscape to be renovated should be evaluated in its entirety and redesigned on paper before much renovation labor goes into it. Because most renovation jobs will occur over a period of time due to time and money constraints, or changes in lifestyles that may be taking place in a family, plans that are broken down into priorities will assure that the various parts of the project are undertaken at the right time. Proper project timing may also be important because there are preferred or better times of year to prune or dig and move certain types of plants.

This book will help you understand more about how plants grow in their environment, and about how to make needed adjustments resulting from that growth. We use a step-by-step approach that progresses from a thorough plant inventory and environmental evaluation to the order in which to remove, prune, or replace plants, and also discuss a renovation calendar or project breakdown.

There may be times during the development of a landscape renovation project when outside help is needed, but most homeowners can do the majority of the planning work themselves. When assistance is needed, it will be available from books and other publications, local nursery and garden center personnel, the county or city Cooperative Extension Service, and professional landscape architects and designers. Even if you're a novice when it comes to landscape design, installation, and maintenance, following the steps in this book in the order suggested can make you look like a pro (Figure 1-9).

2

ANALYZING THE PLANTS IN A LANDSCAPE

When undertaking a landscape renovation project, it is important to determine why the landscape needs changing in order to determine what types of alterations to make and how to make them. This initial step in the renovation project begins with standing back from the landscape and analyzing it as you might if you were driving down the street toward it or pulling into the driveway and facing it.

What is it about the current status of the landscape that makes you feel a renovation project is necessary? Does the front yard look like a jungle? Is there nothing of interest to look at? Do the plants all look as if they are dying?

Next, step from the street into the landscape and look more closely at some of the features you've looked at only from a distance. Are too many plants all growing together (Figure 2-1)? Has one large plant begun to dominate everything (Figure 2-2)? Are all of the plants you look at evergreens with small or inconspicuous fruits or flowers that don't lend color to the landscape? Are the plants covered with insects whose feeding has been slowly draining off the plants' nutrients and killing them? In some cases you may not know the specific causes of plant decline, so seek the help of your extension office or a professional from a local nursery.

As you make both your distant and your close-up analyses, try to put each plant into one of the following categories: an aesthetic or a visual problem, a plant-related problem, a problem caused by a potentially hazardous condition or situation, or no problem at all. Fitting the problems into these categories will help you to improve the current situation and prevent similar problems from occurring in the future (Figure 2-3).

AESTHETIC AND VISUAL PROBLEMS

Many of the most obvious problems in a landscape simply tell the viewer's eye that something is wrong. The landscape just isn't the pretty picture we'd like it to be or it does nothing to complement the house or help it blend in with its surroundings.

A Question of Proportion

What causes landscapes to look "wrong" more quickly than any other feature (except for a yard full of dead or storm-damaged plants) is plants that are out of proportion. They may be out of proportion — either too big or too small — with the house, with other plants in the immediate land-

7

Figure 2-1. In this landscape, too many plants are growing too close together.

Figure 2-2. The plantings at the front of this house are overpowered by the size of the blue spruce — it has grown to the point of distraction and represents a potential hazard.

scape, or even with plants in surrounding landscapes (Figures 2-4 and 2-5).

Fast-growing plants used to landscape around a one-story house will become disproportionate first. This fast growth-rate problem is often compounded either by good care that has pushed the plants to their maximum growth rate, or by negligence — plant sizes could have been kept within more reasonable proportions if persistent pruning had been started when the plants were young.

This out-of-proportion problem is most obvious with plants that have been placed close to the house in the typical foundation planting, and with shade and specimen (frequently evergreen) trees that were planted in the yard in front of the house. It will be less evident for the plants that are further away.

Inappropriate Plants

A more subtle visual problem occurs when plants fail to fit a particular landscape situation, such as the use of plants whose form or texture does not complement the house's architectural style or even surrounding plants (Figure 2-6). As an example, desert plants would not be appropriate in the landscape of a typical New England home.

Color is another example of how plants may fail to fit. Color contrasts can exist between the house and the plants placed close to it. Such features as flower, fruit, or fall leaf color may contrast unpleasantly with the color of the house finish, trim, or shutters. More often the unpleasant color contrast exists between different plants that bloom at the same time. If all of the contrasting plants are still desired in the landscape it may be possible to substitute varieties of the same plant that have differ-

Figure 2-3

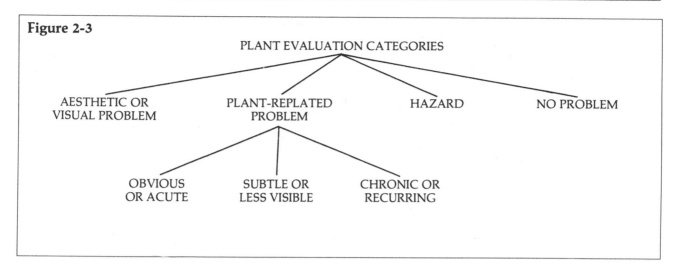

PLANT EVALUATION CATEGORIES

AESTHETIC OR
VISUAL PROBLEM

PLANT-REPLATED
PROBLEM

HAZARD

NO PROBLEM

OBVIOUS
OR ACUTE

SUBTLE OR
LESS VISIBLE

CHRONIC OR
RECURRING

ent colors or bloom times for one of the conflicting plants. In some cases it may even be possible to physically separate the contrasting plants far enough apart so that the contrast is no longer obvious or visible.

Plants can also fail to fit together if their growth rates are very different. If one plant grows much faster than the other plants it can begin to not only visually dominate the other plants, but may even interfere with the growth of the others by competing with them for water and nutrients, or by casting shade which may inhibit their growth.

Design Inadequacies

Another place where landscaping styles or practices from the past (such as foundation plantings mentioned in chapter 1) can continue to cause aesthetic or visual problems, is in the use of formal design. Formal design can be manifest as symmetrical or mirror-image groupings of plants in the foundation planting in front of a house. It can also be seen in the rigid shapes into which many plants are pruned or sheared, or in the soldierlike straight-line plantings that may be part of a foundation planting or form a hedge or screen around a landscape.

Though many houses are still being symmetrically designed, they are no longer necessarily being landscaped with formal designs. These designs impose a very rigid appearance on the house and plants, and can increase plant maintenance if the plants must be constantly pruned or sheared to keep their artificially symmetrical shape (Figure 2-7). Informal designs can be developed for symmetrically shaped houses, and maintaining plants in their natural form with correct height-reduction

Figure 2-4. The dwarf Alberta spruce planted on either side of the doorway are too small in proportion to the rest of the house.

Figure 2-5. Well-maintained and healthy plants, such as those shown above, can quickly outgrow the home they were meant to complement. The house is almost entirely hidden by a crowded and disproportionate landscape.

Figure 2-6. A well-intentioned, but inappropriate landscape. The very narrow evergreens serve to cut the doorway off from the rest of the house. The solution is to move the plantings to the front corners.

Figure 2-7. Straight-line plantings of rigidly sheared evergreens need a great deal of regular maintenance, may not suit the design of your home, and lack seasonal interest.

pruning can greatly decrease maintenance work.

Where plants have been placed in straight-line fashion, adding or moving a few plants so that they are in less formal groupings can easily soften the effect. If the straight-line planting is the typical row of evergreens, include with the rearranged plants groupings of a second, more colorful plant (frequently a flowering deciduous plant). Considerable interest and relief from the monotony of formal design will be added.

The Clutter Factor

For anyone who likes plants it is easy to create an undesirable and cluttered-looking landscape because of one's compulsion to collect one of every plant possible. At the grocery store you pick up one pretty little flowering shrub, at the hardware store's plant sale one or two cute little evergreens, and at the garden center an assortment of new plants that have been introduced this year. Soon your landscape no longer resembles a home environment, but looks more like a mini-arboretum.

If you are inclined to collect or rescue plants, have a special place in a low-visibility area for your collection. The front yard is not the place to stage your initial display. Plantings in the front of the house should be kept to a minimum of three or four species that whenever possible are used in groupings of at least three or five or some other uneven number (Figure 2-8). Wherever possible one or more of the species should be repeated to help give continuity to your design.

If a plant from your collection does especially well, you might consider moving it before it gets

Figure 2-8. Isolated tulips planted on either side of the walkway add nothing to the landscape. The bulbs should be dug up and planted in color-coordinated masses for best effect.

too large to a higher-visibility area for use as an accent or focal point. If the plant is a shrub or perennial try to buy or propagate additional plants so that a grouping can be used.

A Sparse or Disfigured Landscape

One of the major visual problems in many landscapes is actually the opposite of the above — it's a lack of things to look at. All too many landscapes seem to be dominated by evergreens that don't offer the seasonal variation that adds interest to the environment. When looking for plant material try to buy plants that have interest for more than one season, or for longer than a week or two if they only have one-season interest (Figure 2-9). Ask about a plant's flowers — their color, size, longevity, and rebloom potential. Ask about the fruits that follow a plant's flowers — are they showy, are they edible, will they create a litter problem that will increase your maintenance work?

Ask about more subtle ways to introduce color and interest into the landscape. What about a plant's leaves — any seasonal color change or cultivars with different or multicolored leaves (Figure 2-10)? Ask about the bark — what color is it, does it peel off or exfoliate, does it have interesting ridges or corky projections (Figure 2-11)? Even buds can be interesting if they are large and prominent or covered with interesting scales or hairs. Crown shapes and branch patterns of many trees and shrubs can also lend interest to the landscape even if they are deciduous and lose their leaves.

There may be parts of your landscape that have simply worn out. If a lawn area has been heavily trafficked or been used as a ball field by children, portions of the turf may be reduced or nonexistent. Plants, in particular trees, may have been the object of abuse or vandalism. On some trees the damage may consist of broken branches as a result of children swinging on them. On others it may consist of damaged bark from initials being carved into it, lines being tied around it, or items being nailed to it. Trees should not be used as neighborhood bulletin boards or as posts for garage sale signs.

Disagreeable Sights

Another source of aesthetic or visual problems is unsightly views. These views may be on your property, such as a dog run or the garbage can storage area, or may be off your property, such as a

Figure 2-9. The goldenrain tree has multiseasonal interest: flower clusters in the summer followed by interesting fruit pods (above) that are maintained throughout the winter.

How to Tell if Plants Are Dead

One of the most confusing situations for a homeowner is determining whether or not a plant (or plant part) is dead at certain times of the year. The easiest way to tell is to wait until active growth is visible again. If a plant looks dead during the winter, wait until new stem, leaf, and/or flower growth starts in the spring before removing it or possibly improperly pruning it. Even if the same plant has already begun to grow in neighboring locations, wait a few extra weeks before taking any action in case your plant is suffering from some form of stress that has delayed the resumption of its growth.

If you need to know the status of a plant during the winter or while it is dormant, scratch away the bark from a small section of stem in the suspected area. Look for a layer of green tissue under the bark. This tissue is the cambium layer, the place where new cell growth will originate. If this layer is not green, but tan or brown in color, the cambium area has died and no new growth will take place in that area. Continue to scratch off small bark areas progressing down a stem until you get to an area where the cambium is green again. This will distinguish the living from the dead stem tissue and will serve as a guide for where to prune, or will allow you to estimate how much of the plant is still alive and whether or not you should keep the plant.

There is no point in planting, moving, or performing maintenance work on plants that are no longer alive. And there certainly is no reason to leave dead plants in a landscape where they will only detract from the overall appearance of the landscape and will be potential hazards. ∎

◄ **This evergreen euonymus suffered winter-kill because of its exposed location, but it is starting to make new growth at the base. Don't be deceived by the weak looking leaves and stems that make it appear dead.**

neighbor's messy yard or a recreational vehicle parked near your patio. Whatever the reason, with additional landscaping, whether with plant or non-plant structures, many unsightly views can be reduced, hidden, or one's attention diverted from them. Be sure to consider all views from within your house, from within your landscape, and from outside your landscape when adding plants and structures (Figure 2-12).

PLANT-RELATED PROBLEMS

Landscape renovation may be desirable or necessary due to plant-related problems. Most of these problems can be placed in one or more of three categories that will help you understand them better: obvious or acute plant-related problems; subtle or less visible plant-related problems; and chronic or recurring plant-related problems.

Acute Problems

Obvious or acute plant-related problems are generally the most visible problems. Perhaps the most common and obvious are dead plants that have never been removed from the landscape (Figure 2-13). Other evident problems are bare lawn areas where foot traffic compaction has lowered the soil's oxygen content below a level that will sustain the turf grass, and plants that are rapidly dying due to acute disease, insect, or environmental complications.

For most of these problems some form of immediate attention is justified. Dead or dying plants can be removed, compacted soil can be aerated, and plant pest problems can be treated. Before replacements are planted, if replanting is justified, a good evaluation of the cause of the trouble should be made. Site adjustment work or the selection of more appropriate plants may be necessary.

Subtle Problems

Subtle or less visible plant-related problems are ones that may have developed over a long period of time and whose manifestation took longer to develop or was less apparent. Examples of such problems include dense shade that developed as a tree grew, resulting in areas where turf grasses won't grow; salt spray or wash from the use of deicing salts on roads that caused gradual soil compaction and plant damage; and flowering ornamentals that declined in flower production or are no longer flowering (or fruiting) at all.

The solutions to the subtle or less visible plant-related problems are often less dramatic than for the obvious problems, and may or may not involve plant removal. In the case of the dense tree shade, some of the tree's lower limbs can be removed to allow more light to penetrate, or a more shade-tolerant grass variety or ground cover can be planted under it. With road-deicing salt damage, a different material can be used on the roads, the compacted soil can be treated with gypsum, the soil can be heavily watered to leach away extra salts, and the plants can be physically washed off to remove any salt residues.

Where plant growth has begun to decline, again as evidenced by a decrease in flower and/or fruit production, or where leaves have gotten smaller and/or lighter green in color, or fall color has failed to develop, more than one factor may be contributing to the problem. As with the above shade example, the plants may be receiving too little light. They also may have been improperly pruned or fertilized, developed a disease problem, or several years of environmental stress may have weakened the plant.

As you can see, many factors need to be considered. In some cases they can be corrected, in others the plants may need to be removed and possibly replaced. Recent research has even revealed that some plants are "allergic" to other plants and cannot grow in their vicinity due to toxic substances secreted by the "poisoning" plant's root system, a phenomenon called allelopathy.

Recurring Problems

The third category of chronic or recurring plant-related problems can be the most taxing with regard to landscape maintenance requirements (Figure 2-14). The three most common examples of chronic plant-related problems are plants that cause litter, plants that get the same insect/disease problems or problem conditions every year, and

Figure 2-10. This variegated euonymus adds color interest to the landscape because it has green and white leaves.

Figure 2-11. Consider even the bark of a plant when designing a landscape. In this case, the bark of a crape myrtle has interesting color variations.

Why Plants Fail to Flower or Fruit

A major frustration for homeowners is to have purchased and planted trees, shrubs, vines, and assorted perennials and annuals only to find that the flowers and/or fruit never develop or at best develop poorly. Homeowners are often quick to blame the weather or some other factor beyond their control, but with a little knowledge of flower and fruit production many of their disappointments can be averted.

One major reason that a flowering plant will not bloom or will have fewer flowers than expected is insufficient light intensity and duration. Most outdoor flowering plants (unless they specifically flower better in the shade — there are many exceptions) need a minimum of six hours of direct sunlight in order to set large numbers of flower buds. If the plant is installed in too shady a location, or if shade has developed over the years as trees have grown, light intensity and duration may be inadequate. In cases like this the plants will need to be moved or the shade intensity reduced.

Another environmental condition that can prevent or reduce flowering is a summer drought followed by a warm, wet fall. Under these conditions the plant is tricked into thinking it is spring. The buds break, flowering begins, and then cold temperatures kill the buds or flowers. Little can be done in this situation other than to prune off the dead growth.

Late spring frosts can also kill buds and flowers that have begun to grow. This problem can be intensified by premature warm weather in late winter. If conditions such as these occur frequently in your area, later-blooming varieties and cultivars should be used, or the plants should be installed in microclimates with more buffered conditions.

Cultural practices are often to blame when flowering declines or stops. Flowering will be reduced on many deciduous shrubs as they age if the old wood isn't periodically pruned out and new wood that will produce more flowers allowed to develop. And pruning done at the wrong time of year may remove next season's flower buds.

Another cultural practice that may be at fault is fertilization. Over- and under-fertilization, as well as using the wrong kind of fertilizer, can affect flowering. If a high-nitrogen lawn fertilizer is used on flowering shrubs, they may produce lush vegetative (stem and leaf) growth at the expense of flowers.

Too much and too little water can also affect flowering. Under drought conditions plants may drop or shed flower buds in order to conserve water, and under excessively moist conditions buds may rot, or certain diseases may develop that can reduce flowering. Disease problems that affect flowering can ▶

plants that are constantly in need of pruning.

Plant litter may be in the form of large leaves that drop in the fall and are slow to decompose or are cumbersome to rake up. The litter may be fruit that falls or small branches that constantly break off and must be collected (Figure 2-15). In cases such as these, there is generally little that can be done except to remove the plant(s) if the maintenance work that is required becomes too unreasonable.

Plants that have recurrent disease or insect problems can be removed altogether, they can be removed and replaced with more disease or insect tolerant or resistant varieties if possible, or regular pest control measures can be instituted if they won't increase maintenance too much.

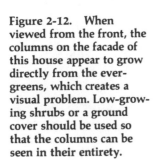
Figure 2-12. When viewed from the front, the columns on the facade of this house appear to grow directly from the evergreens, which creates a visual problem. Low-growing shrubs or a ground cover should be used so that the columns can be seen in their entirety.

▲ A late spring freeze killed the flowers on this early spring-blooming star magnolia, and thus diminished the only real seasonal interest of this tree.

occur under other environmental conditions as well.

Some plants, especially trees, need to attain a certain age or stage of maturity before they will flower. And with some plants their flowering is cyclical or alternating — heavy in some years, and light in the following years.

All of the above factors that affect flowering will also affect fruiting. If flower production is reduced or is nonexistent, fruit production will be similarly affected. But there are additional reasons that plants may fail to fruit. One of the basic facts to remember is that most fruits form only as a result of pollination of the flowers. Anything that affects pollination will, therefore, also affect fruiting. Although most plants are self-pollinating, there are those that must be cross pollinated. Some plants don't produce enough pollen to pollinate themselves, others produce pollen at a time when the female part of the flower isn't receptive, or produce pollen that isn't compatible with the female part of its own flowers.

One special case of mandatory cross-pollination involves dioecious plants, which have male and female flowers on separate plants. A male of the species must be within pollinating distance of a female in order for fruit to form. In some cases where cross-pollination is required, only very specific plants can serve as cross-pollinators. These specific pollen providers may be other cultivars of the same plant, or may even be different species of plants.

Even if all of the above cross-pollination requirements are met, plants may still fail to set fruit if the environment is adverse. Heat, cold, and drought can kill pollen, and inadequate wind or insect activity may fail to get the pollen transferred.

Even if pollination is successful, fruit may still fail to form if the environment is adverse. Here the most common problem is inadequate moisture that either results in fruit drop or undersized fruits. Before buying flowering and fruiting plants be sure to find out all of their requirements so as to insure successful flower and fruit production. ■

For plants that are constantly in need of pruning, the renovation decision again relates to the maintenance demands. If the plants lend themselves to renovation or renewal pruning (rather drastic size reduction), they should be pruned in this manner. Start natural shape-maintaining pruning as soon as they begin to regrow (see chapter 5). This will greatly reduce their growth rate and the amount of overall pruning that will be necessary.

If the plants will not respond well to renovation pruning, they may need to be thinned back temporarily or removed and replaced with smaller or slower-growing species. If the plants had been serving as a screen, a better solution may be to replace them with a permanent fixture such as a fence.

Figure 2-13.   Dead landscape elements (lawn and a couple of yews) contribute nothing to it and should be removed.

Figure 2-14. Cool- and warm-season grasses combined in the same lawn have created a chronic problem. Not only does each type of grass have different maintenance requirements, but each thrives at a different time of the year. As a result, the lawn never looks acceptable.

Figure 2-15. Tree fruit can create a litter problem. In this case, fallen sweet gum balls.

HAZARDS IN THE LANDSCAPE

Unless a shrub has particularly large and menacing thorns, or a tree has a broken branch that is hanging precariously over a sidewalk, it is difficult for people to envision plants or other elements in a landscape as being hazardous. With a few suggestions about what to look for, and a close and critical eye, however, most homeowners will find one or more current or potential hazards in their home landscapes.

One of the most obvious hazards exists where plants have grown large and block or obscure something (Figure 2-16). A large shrub by the entrance to a house may cover the house's street number — creating a dilemma for emergency personnel (police, fire, ambulance) who are looking for the house. Obscured numbers can also be a problem if delivery people or even invited guests cannot find them (Figure 2-17). For the sake of the mailman try not to create an obstacle course on the way to your mailbox.

Large plants at the end of a driveway or on the edge of the street may obscure a motorist's view when the motorist is trying to back out of a driveway or pull into traffic. Those little shrubs that were planted on either side of the driveway fifteen years ago may now be the cause of a serious accident. If you look around several landscapes you are bound to find other examples of this kind that create potentially hazardous situations.

Utility Lines

Plants create another type of hazard when they interfere with utility lines. The two most common examples are street tree branches growing into overhead power lines and tree roots growing into water and sewer lines. In the case of street tree branches, utility companies have legal rights to easement areas around the lines where they can clear branches away. In many cases because of the amount of time required or difficulty getting to the branches, however, pruning methods employed by the utility companies are not as technically correct or as aesthetically appealing as they could be. A sad fact is that much of this pruning would be unnecessary if we were more careful when planting trees near utility lines (Figure 2-18). In the case of street trees, we need to look up when we plant the trees to see what they might interfere with in the future.

Many of the old street trees that have been severely pruned and deformed should be removed. If new trees are planted in their place, they should be replaced with species whose mature height will remain below the lines, or with trees positioned so that the spread of their crown stays under or away from the lines.

In the case of trees whose roots grow into water and sewer lines, many of these are weak-wooded species of trees (swamp, water, or silver maples; poplars; willows) whose roots, despite being routed out of the lines or killed back with chemicals, will continue to invade the lines. The best solution is to remove these nuisance trees.

Before any trees are planted all underground utility and water and sewer lines should be located. Simply call the utility companies and ask them to come flag where the lines run. Trees, other plants, and even structures should be kept a considerable distance from these underground lines. As with

Figure 2-16. A very dangerous situation exists when plants are allowed to overgrow the area around a stop sign. When a car is stopped at this sign, the driver cannot see oncoming traffic because of the plant growth.

Figure 2-17. A hazard is created when plants are allowed to block an entrance — the door then becomes inaccessible, it will be dark at night, and street numbers or signs are obscured.

Figure 2-18. The sugar maple shown here has too large a mature height to be planted under utility lines, which makes its proximity to the wires unsafe.

Figure 2-19. The juniper shown here was planted to cover an unsightly manhole cover, but now it blocks the flow of water into the storm sewer and acts to catch leaves and debris, creating more maintenance chores. Better to remove it altogether.

the overhead utility lines, legal easements exist that will allow a utility company to dig up or prune back plants, or dig up paving or structures that interfere with their servicing activities. Other items to avoid blocking include storm sewers, fire plugs, traffic signs, utility meters, and for those in rural locations, septic systems, leaching fields, and wells (Figure 2-19).

Many trees have shallow root systems that often surface due to low-soil moisture content or compaction, or simply because of how they grow. These roots can create a hazard by heaving up the pavement. If the paving is a sidewalk, the roots can cause a very dangerous situation for pedestrians, and an often impassable situation for someone in a wheelchair.

Trees that are planted near paving should have deep roots, or should be set a considerable distance back from the paving (Figure 2-20). Paving should never be placed over the top of roots that have surfaced. If it is installed near existing trees, stay as far away from them as possible, both to avoid physically damaging the roots and to avoid covering the roots with a nonporous material, thereby removing the trees' water source.

Tree roots often surface also under the drip line of lawn trees, creating hazards for mowing. Though the lawn mower may injure the roots by removing bark and sometimes woody tissue, this type of damage does not kill as many trees as are killed when lawn mowers hit the trees themselves. Lawn mower wounds at the base of a tree remove stem tissue. This type of wound can kill the tree through starvation by preventing food movement down from the leaves to the roots. It can also indirectly kill the tree by serving as an entry port for insect and disease organisms (Figure 2-21).

Damage From Climbing Plants

Another type of damage from plant roots results from the roots of climbing vines growing into tree bark, the wood of buildings, or even the mortar of masonry walls. Care should be exercised in removing the vines. To best minimize damage it is better to sever these vines from their roots and let the vines die before pulling the vines away from the trees or structures they are attached to. Vines can also damage trees as they twine up them. They can have a girdling effect that potentially interferes with the downward movement of food from the

Figure 2-20. The chances of accident or injury are greatly increased when pavement is heaved by surfacing tree roots.

Figure 2-21. The lawn mower wound at the base of this tree has expanded and is an easy entry port for insects and diseases.

Figure 2-22. This silver maple has developed a narrow branch crotch angle — an unsafe situation. A big wind or storm could cause a chain reaction in which one or both of these branches are ripped away, thereby damaging the main branch as well.

Figure 2-23. Tree roots can be damaged and weakened by road construction. The two trees shown fell onto a house.

Figure 2-24. Spikes or thorns represent a very real hazard to children and animals. Each homeowner will have to decide if such disadvantages outweigh the known benefits of such plants. Shown here is a honey locust.

leaves to the roots. This blockage, as mentioned above, can result in the slow starvation of the trees.

Weakened, Damaged, or Harmful Plants

Trees that have been weakened by natural or artificial causes are subtle, and often overlooked, potential hazards. Tree limbs that have been partially torn away by strong winds, lightning strikes, or ice or snow loads may eventually fall once the remaining branch tissues have died. Trees that have had the major branches severely cut back (an extremely unsound and unnecessary practice in virtually any landscape situation, see page 37) or that naturally form narrow branch crotch angles can have branches easily split off or pulled away from the tree (Figure 2-22).

Major attacks from insects or diseases can slowly weaken a plant to the point that it will die or fall over. These pest attacks can be especially dangerous where trees of the same species have roots that have naturally grafted together. This natural grafting forms a convenient passageway from one plant to another through which certain disease organisms can move.

Roots can also be weakened or destroyed by construction damage, road cuts, paving and curbing, grade changes, underground utility work, or installation of in-ground swimming pools (Figure 2-23). Construction work should be kept as far away as possible from plant roots, tree trunks, and limbs to avoid causing any damage that might kill the plants outright or provide access to insect and disease organisms.

Figure 2-25. Flower petals that fall on a wet sidewalk can be very slippery.

Plants in themselves can even be hazardous because of the way portions of them grow or substances they may contain or produce. Many plants have thorns or spikes that can be hazardous to children playing near them (Figure 2-24). Others have poisonous parts, mainly fruits and leaves, that can cause reactions ranging from mild dermatitis to stomach poisoning and even death. Lists of poisonous plants can be obtained from reference books, from the Cooperative Extension Service, and from many physicians. If in doubt regarding the poisonous potential of a plant or plant part, call the Poison Control Center in Atlanta.

Many plants also drop parts that can be hazardous (as mentioned earlier with regard to chronic plant-related problems). Large fruit can fall on someone passing beneath a tree, or flower petals may fall on a wet sidewalk and become very slippery underfoot.

The Landscape Owner's Responsibility

Many examples of nonplant hazards also exist in the landscape. Insufficient night lighting can cause problems as guests try to determine house street numbers or find their way to the front door. Metal edging used to outline beds often sticks above ground and may be tripped over or get caught in the lawn mower. People also trip over uneven paving and hoses stretched out to water gardens, and may fall if there are uneven surfaces or holes in the lawn.

We have only to look around a few landscapes to find many plant and nonplant hazards that can be dangerous to family members, guests, service and emergency personnel, and other visitors (Figure 2-25). With the cost of liability insurance today, it is vital to remove as many obvious or potential hazards as possible from our landscapes and homes.

NO PROBLEMS

Some plants in your landscape will have no identifiable problems — they won't fit into any of the above-mentioned categories. With these plants, as with those that do fit into specific problem categories, it is now important to analyze them relative to their condition, which will be discussed in the following chapter.

3

EVALUATING THE CONDITION OF EXISTING PLANT MATERIAL

The analytical exercise prescribed in the previous chapter was designed to make you more aware of the components of your landscape and their impact on you, your environment, other plants and structural elements whose space they share. Now that you have identified any problem areas contributing to the need for renovation work in your landscape, it is time to analyze more closely the physical condition of the plants.

To help organize this next stage, use these three basic plant condition categories: plants in good condition, plants in marginal condition, and plants in poor condition. By placing each plant in your landscape into one of these categories you will be better able to decide how to deal with each plant — whether to keep, move, prune, fertilize, or discard it (Figure 3-1). Evaluate your plants according to the criteria found on the pages that follow, then construct a chart like the one on page 25 that will serve as your guide during the renovation process.

PLANTS IN GOOD CONDITION

With luck many of the plants in your landscape are in good condition so that you will be able to keep and use them. How do you determine if they are in good condition? This takes knowing what a healthy, vigorous plant looks like for each species in your landscape.

If you are well acquainted with a particular plant, you should be able to tell from various characteristics what its current condition is. Is leaf size and color appropriate? For deciduous plants, the time it leafs out in the spring and drops its leaves in the fall may be an indicator of its internal (physiological) condition. If the plant is a flowering ornamental, are an adequate number of flowers (and possibly fruits) produced at the right time of year and in the right color? Is the plant's rate of growth adequate? Is the plant able to withstand attacks by known insect and disease pests?

It is important to collect as much information as possible on the above-ground growth of the plant. We are rarely able, unfortunately, to determine root condition without damaging the plant, yet this can often indicate the condition of the plant better than any other part.

If you are unfamiliar with a plant, consult reference books on plant material, request the help of your local Cooperative Extension Service and garden center personnel, or visit local gardens or arboretums that display plant material. If some of the plants in your landscape grow in the landscapes

Figure 3-1

```
                            PLANT CONDITION


        GOOD                    MARGINAL                    POOR


   KEEP IN    MOVE         KEEP IN    MOVE    REMOVE        REMOVE
   PLACE                   PLACE


                                              REPLACE?      REPLACE?
```

Figure 3-2. Slight differences in microclimate have caused the decline of half of this landscape. In the top photo, it can be seen that the yews and evergreen azaleas facing the northeast (on the left) are doing well and could stay. But those same shrubs on the northwest side of the home (on the right), have suffered decline because of cold winter winds and drying summer exposure. The best solution is to replace the planting so that both sides match, although the plants on the northeast could be moved and used elsewhere in the landscape. The replacement plants, in the bottom photo, are redtwig dogwood and chamaecyparis.

Plant Evaluation Chart					
PLANT	**LOCATION**	**SIZE**	**PROBLEM**	**PLANT CONDITION**	**ACTION**

Possible codes

Location: F - front, B - back, S - side, or N - north, S - south, etc.

Size: Actual height & spread, or TT - tall trees, SS - small shrub, V- vine, etc.

Problem: A - aesthetic, P - plant-related, H - hazard, N - no problem.

Plant Condition: G - good, M - marginal, P - poor.

Action: K - keep in place, M - move, RM - remove, R - replace, also F - fertilize, P - prune, M - mulch, etc.

Figure 3-3. A flowering crabapple in fine condition, but positioned wrong because it takes up too much space in front of the house and blocks the front door. If possible, it should be moved to a better location when the tree is dormant.

Figure 3-4. This Japanese holly was pruned too late in the summer. New growth stimulated by pruning was later killed by an early fall frost.

of your neighbors, compare your plants with theirs.

As you view the plants in other settings keep in mind that very slight environmental or microclimatic differences from one location to another can have a significant impact on the growth of a plant. Examples of varied conditions include sunny versus shady exposures, well-drained versus constantly wet or puddled soil, and windy exposures versus calm or protected areas (Figure 3-2).

For those plants you determine to be in good condition, check to see whether or not you have identified them as part of one of the three problem areas described in chapter 2 (aesthetic or visual problems, plant-related problems, hazards). If you have, there may be many options available to you. For example, if a plant is a visual problem you may be able to keep it in the same location if you prune it or thin it out. Or you may be able to add companion color plants to it depending on what your analysis reveals.

You may decide that one of your plants in good condition is not in the best location, and that it could be better used somewhere else in your landscape (Figure 3-3). This will necessitate moving it at an appropriate time (see chapter 6). Or you may decide that the plant can no longer be used effectively in your landscape, and so you remove it and either give it away, sell it, or destroy it.

For all plants that are in good condition which you intend to either keep in place in your landscape, or move to another location, set up mainte-

Figure 3-5. Shrubs (junipers) in marginal condition. The amount of foliage in the lower area has been reduced by age and shade.

nance schedules for them. Preventative maintenance schedules that tell you when to fertilize, prune, and treat for pest problems, if adhered to, can reduce the overall amount of maintenance time you must devote to your landscape (see chapters 6 and 7).

Remember that you want to keep the plants healthy, yet you do not want to overstimulate their growth as is often done by overfertilizing lawn grasses at the wrong time of year, which subsequently increases the need for mowing. We can also overstimulate trees and shrubs, thereby adding extra maintenance work or sometimes causing the plants to put out weak or rank growth that may have less resistance to pest or environmental problems (winter cold extremes, dehydrating winter winds, or summer droughts; Figure 3-4).

PLANTS IN MARGINAL CONDITION

Some of the plants in your landscape may be in marginal condition. One example of marginal-condition plants includes those that are getting older and that through repeated pruning have lost their lower foliage or have died out at the bottom (Figure 3-5). Another example is plants that are no longer producing as many flowers as they once did (due to improper pruning, lack of fertilizer, or increased shade from surrounding plants). Still

another example is plants whose leaves or other parts frequently sustain damage from insect and disease pests.

With marginal-condition plants the decision of whether or not to keep the plants will be more difficult to make than for plants that are either in good or in poor condition. You must weigh the costs of labor and supplies involved in rejuvenating the plants to acceptable condition (through pruning or fertilizing) as compared to the costs involved in removing, and possibly replacing, the plants. Also consider how long a period of time your remedial work will keep that marginal plant functional or effective in the landscape. If a lot of work will be involved, and the plant will probably need to be removed in a year or two anyway, the remedial work probably isn't justified and the plant should be removed (Figure 3-6).

Never assume that because plants have been removed from a location that new plants should go in that area. Our landscapes tend to be overplanted, not underplanted. Often if you leave a location from which a plant has been removed vacant for half a year or so you will find that you do not miss it visually; unless it was contributing to environmental modification around your house, such as summer shade or winter wind barrier, you really have no reason to replace it.

If a plant was classified in your analysis as being a hazard, it obviously should not be replaced with the same plant unless that plant's growth is kept under better control or unless a dwarf or slower-

Figure 3-6. The Japanese hollies shown are in marginal condition because of neglect and possible competition from the grass. The center shrub should be removed and the other two pruned naturally, fertilized, and the grassed area converted into a mulched bed.

Figure 3-7. The air conditioning unit shown above is being shaded by the surrounding plants, which keeps it cooler and increases its efficiency.

growing variety is used. If you do decide to replace plants that you remove, and your analysis showed that a disease or insect organism weakened the plant, do not use the same species or a related species that is susceptible, unless you can find a resistant or tolerant cultivar or variety.

PLANTS IN POOR CONDITION

Some of the plants in your landscape will undoubtedly be in poor condition, since plants of declining growth are one of the major reasons that people undertake renovation projects. With plants in poor condition it is generally not difficult to decide to remove them (for contributing factors see chapter 4). If you consider replacing them with new plants, consider how pest problems and environmental factors, such as too much shade or potential snow damage in winter, will impact on replacement species.

Another consideration when removing plants should be how the plant's removal will influence the growth of other plants in the landscape, the environment around your house, and possibly even the wildlife that may frequent your landscape. If a shade tree that is adjacent to your house on the south or west side is removed, its absence will increase the impact of summer heat on your house. This increase in heat may then have to be dealt with by the installation of an air-conditioning unit. If air conditioning was already present, the plant may have actually been keeping the air-conditioning system cooler so that it worked more efficiently (Figure 3-7).

The shade tree's removal may also increase the light intensity for plants that were growing under it or in its shade. For some plants this may improve their growth, especially if they were deciduous flowering ornamentals. For other plants, however, such as shade-requiring perennials, the decreased shade may interfere with their healthy growth or may even lead to their death.

If a plant is removed because it was killed or badly damaged by a particular insect, the plant's removal may mean that the insect problem will disappear if the insect was very host-specific. In some cases, however, the insect will begin to attack other species of plants that it preferred less while the more vulnerable plant was growing, but which

will now serve as adequate food sources. In a similar fashion, some plants are affected by disease organisms that require two very different plant species as alternate hosts in order to complete their life cycle. If one host is removed the other may be able to return to healthy growth because the disease organism will die out unless other alternate hosts are growing in neighboring landscapes.

The examples given here show the complex interactions that exist in landscapes. Each landscape is a series of small microclimates or environments, and when a plant is removed it can greatly alter a landscape by changing one or more of those microclimates. The impact of any renovation project to the existing landscape should be considered as the new landscaping is being designed. Try to use the best aspects and plants in the existing landscape to the maximum benefit of the new landscape.

4

FACTORS CONTRIBUTING TO PLANT DECLINE AND POOR GROWTH

Landscape plants may begin to grow poorly or to decline for a number of reasons. More often than not, several factors have had a compounding effect on a plant's condition. For example, on first inspection a plant may appear to be dying from disease. Upon closer observation of the plant and its microenvironment, however, you may find that damage from a lawn mower, coupled with a utility company cutting through the root system, have combined to weaken the plant. The disease you see is only a secondary pathogen (an organism that causes disease) that might not have been able to attack the plant had other factors not weakened or predisposed it to disease.

Now that chapters 2 and 3 have helped you to analyze your landscape's problems, and to evaluate the condition of existing plant material, it is time, before getting out the shovel or pruning shears, to determine why the plants that were judged to be in only marginal or poor condition have deteriorated to that point. By looking at contributing factors you may be able to rejuvenate marginal plants or to keep the new plants that you will be adding to your landscape from also declining or growing poorly.

THE QUALITY OF PLANT MATERIALS

If possible, start by thinking back to the quality and condition of the trees and shrubs when you first saw them. If you were the one who originally purchased and installed the plants, then you may remember whether they were good-quality, healthy, vigorous plants purchased from a reputable nursery or garden center. Or were the plants bargains from a discount center or from a grocery store that neglected them and then heavily discounted them in order to sell them? Were they divisions from a neighbor's overgrown plant that were in poor condition when you planted them?

Some bargain or neglected plants will beat the odds and grow into vigorous plants, especially with a little extra care. But you generally get what you pay for, and it may simply take several years before the plants die.

PLANT AGE

One of the most common reasons for the decline of trees and shrubs in a landscape is simply old age. For some reason most people have the notion that any plants, other than annual garden flowers and vegetables, have an infinite life and should never need to be replaced.

In reality this is far from correct — plants, like other living organisms, have average predictable life spans. Even if a tree has the genetic potential to live for a hundred years, the environmental conditions that impact on it, and the cultural care it may or may not receive, will help to determine whether or not that potential life span will be met, lengthened, or shortened. It's a sad fact that in our current stressful urban street environments, many trees that might have had long life spans under average conditions rarely survive for more than ten to fifteen years.

What types of environmental conditions shorten the life spans of trees and shrubs? Deicing salt washed from a road or sidewalk, lightning strikes, grade changes that alter the water table level, and numerous other factors which will be elaborated on later in the chapter.

A similar list of nonexistent or negligent cultural practices could also contribute to a shortened life span, including lack of water and fertilizer, misapplied herbicides, and staking or guying wires left in place too long. Again, many of these items will also be described in further detail.

In the case of many of the environmental changes, we may or may not be able to influence or change them. Many cultural practices are within our ability to change, and in so doing we can greatly add to the longevity of our landscape plants.

Figure 4-1. An example of a tree planted in the wrong location. A flowering dogwood prefers moist soil and shade from other trees. Because it was planted in dry, compacted soil and is exposed to full sun and dry winds, its leaves scorch and wilt. This plant will never thrive under such conditions.

INAPPROPRIATE PLANT CHOICES OR PLACEMENT

A very common factor contributing to plant decline is the use of plants that are poorly adapted to the conditions under which they are forced to grow. In native environments plants grow where they do because they find suitable niches in which temperature, amount of sunlight, soil-moisture

Short-Lived Versus Long-Lived Plants

Frequently included with the description of a tree or shrub will be the phrase "short-lived" or "long-lived." This distinction refers to a combination of the genetic age potential of the plant with the realistic life span that might be expected under typical growing conditions.

Both short-lived and long-lived plants have a place in the landscape, each with advantages and disadvantages that should be weighed before selecting one over the other. Potential life span will be of greater importance in selecting trees than shrubs, because trees usually represent a greater monetary investment than shrubs, and because trees are generally functional for a longer time and often make a bolder statement in the landscape.

In general a short-lived tree is one that is fast-growing (silver maple), weak-wooded (willow), and less resistant to disease (Lombardy poplar) than a long-lived tree. Short-lived trees often have root systems that will seek and block water and sewer lines, creating maintenance problems. The often twiggy and erratic growth pattern of their crown, and their greater susceptibility to insect and disease problems can also add to maintenance demands.

Short-lived trees are generally cheaper for the wholesale nursery to grow, and therefore are usually less expensive for the homeowner to buy. They can serve very effectively in the landscape as fast-growing, short-term screens (no more than ten to fifteen years), or as temporary shade while a slower-growing, but longer-lived, tree is getting established.

A long-lived tree is generally a slower-growing species with stronger wood, fewer maintenance demands, and generally a higher price tag. Though it may serve as a poor shade tree in a barren new subdivision where quick shade is desired by homeowners who plan to own their houses for only a few years before moving elsewhere, it may be very desirable for a large lot in an open area away from the house. A long-lived tree may also serve as a replacement tree for a short-lived tree that is beginning to outgrow its functional usefulness.

Whenever you select a tree for a landscape situation, consider all of the above before making your selection. There are acceptable short- and long-lived species of trees for just about any function or location. But don't let the price of the tree alone determine your decision. ■

◄ A short-lived species of tree — a Lombardy poplar — that has weak branches and a fast growth rate.

▲ A long-lived species of tree — a red oak — that has strong branches, a slow growth rate, and an attractive mature appearance.

Figure 4-2. The Norway maple shown at right has scorched and fallen leaves because it is growing in very dry soil and is positioned too close to paved areas that radiate heat onto its crown. The tree should be moved while it is still small.

Figure 4-3. This euonymus (a broad-leaved evergreen) has suffered winter kill and leaf desiccation because it is in a windy, exposed spot.

content, and other factors promote good growth.

When we plant trees and shrubs we frequently pay no attention to the natural conditions they favor, but instead plant them wherever we want. A tree that needs well-aerated, moist soil in a shady location will have great difficulty growing at all, let alone establishing itself, in a sunny location with dry, compacted soil (Figure 4-1). Unfortunately this is all too frequently what we try to impose on plants, and then we wonder why they struggle or die. Even the best cultural practices often can't make up for improper growing conditions.

The most common examples of environmental condition mismatches are listed below.

- Using plants from warmer hardiness zones in areas where the average minimum winter temperature drops too low.
- Using plants that need full sun in the shade or vice versa.
- Using acid-loving plants (such as azaleas or rhododendrons) in only slightly acid or even alkaline soils. Under these conditions the unfavorable soil pH keeps essential nutrients from being available or makes the wrong nutrients too available.
- Using plants that need deep, rich, well-aerated soil in compacted, often poor quality subsoil.
- Using plants that need a fair amount, or an even supply of, moisture in dry soils or in soils whose moisture content varies greatly (Figure 4-2).
- Using plants that need well-aerated soil in areas

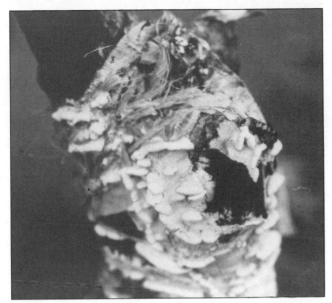

Figure 4-4. Tree wrap that's left in place too long holds excess water against the bark, which could then begin to rot and support the growth of decay fungus, as evidenced above.

Figure 4-6. An improperly pruned tree: long stubs left in this way will die back and serve as entry ports for insects and diseases.

Figure 4-5. The guy wires used on the tree above have been left in place too long and are girdling the tree. The swelling above the guying has been caused by food attempting to translocate from the leaves down to feed the roots, but its movement is blocked by the wires. The roots will slowly starve, and the tree eventually die — a needless situation.

Minimizing Winter Damage

A natural phenomenon that seems to be occurring more frequently in recent years is periods of unusually cold winter weather. A homeowner can't do anything about the severe low temperatures and drying winds, but there are measures that can be taken in colder climates to winterize plants and reduce the amount of damage that may occur.

The first step is to know the orientation (compass points) of your landscape. The greatest amount of injury will occur generally from the southwest to the northwest quadrant. On a southwestern exposure the major problem is uneven heating of tree trunks that can cause the bark to split open. On a northwestern exposure the major problem is the cold, dry winds that desiccate plant leaves and stems.

How should you react to these conditions? When adding new plants, avoid putting thin-barked trees facing southwest, or alternatively, wrap their bark in the winter. Remove the wrap in the spring so that the trunk's growth won't be restricted. Put only very cold-hardy plants facing northwest, and in particular avoid using broadleaf evergreens unless they are especially hardy. Plants are assigned hardiness-zone ratings, so for insurance select plants with a rating for a zone at least one rating colder than where you live. Many plants have several forms or cultivars, some of which may be hardier than others — you should be able to get the type of plant you want with more cold tolerance genetically built in.

If vulnerable plants already exist in exposed locations, and you have seen them damaged in the winter, move them to more sheltered or less exposed locations if possible. If they can't be moved, several cultural measures can help to winterize them.

During late summer and early fall, water the soil if conditions are dry. After the first freeze or killing frost, apply fertilizer that can stimulate additional root growth, and apply a layer of mulch to help keep the soil temperature a bit warmer. In some areas shrubs will benefit from being surrounded by a barrier that reduces the wind's impact. Even though snow is a good insulator against cold and should generally be left covering plants, snow or ice can physically break certain plants, so they may need to be covered with a protective structure. Never shake a plant to remove ice—if the plant tissue itself is frozen, shaking can cause the plant to break. The ice should be allowed to melt away naturally.

Survey your landscape for the plants that seem to show damage after a severe winter and make whatever planting or cultural adjustments you can to help save them. ■

---

where water drains away slowly or tends to puddle or stand for extended periods of time.
- Using deciduous plants with thin leaf blades, or broadleaf evergreens, in exposed, windy locations where their leaves are subjected to constant desiccation (Figure 4-3).

The list could continue, but these are the major mismatches. When shopping for plants, find out what conditions they prefer. If the location in which you had intended to use the plant lacks these conditions, and if you can't do anything to make them more favorable, then look for a different plant whose requirements match the existing conditions. Or as an alternative, find another location for that plant you just have to have.

People often feel that if they use plants that are native (found growing naturally) to an area, the plants will automatically do well. This is a major misconception, because any time man has impacted a planting location the natural conditions have been altered and an artificial environment has been created. Just because a certain tree grows naturally in a wooded area a block away from your homesite doesn't mean that the same tree can survive at your location. Your site may have been transformed into a location where the topsoil and leaf litter were removed, where the natural drainage patterns were altered, or where the thinning of trees during construction has created too sunny a planting site.

In many "artificial" planting sites, introduced (meaning non-native) species will often do better. But here again, native or introduced, each tree and shrub has its own preferred microenvironment. Match their needs and the trees and shrubs should flourish. Put them in harsh environments and watch them die, in some cases slowly as food reserves are used up, in some cases quickly as the plants find nothing that they can do to acclimatize.

IMPROPER CULTIVATION

It is easy to blame the decline of plants in our landscapes on improper planting techniques and improper or negligent maintenance or cultural practices. The proper techniques and practices will

Why Tree Topping is an Undesirable Practice

Old habits can be hard to break, but one practice that exists in the tree-care industry must be changed — topping, heading-back, stubbing, dehorning, or pollarding trees. Regardless of the name used, the practice does not stimulate healthy tree growth, and can turn trees into potential hazards. Unless the practice is stopped we will continue to destroy existing trees and harm future trees.

Topping involves removing or severely cutting back large branches so that large stubs are left. The practice is akin to flat-top shearing a hedge. It is a cosmetic measure at best, and in general greatly increases a tree's maintenance requirements and pest problems. There are good reasons to remove or prune branches from trees, but the key words are *good* and *prune*. Dead or unhealthy branches or limbs that interfere with overhead utility lines should be removed. Growth that interferes with vehicular visibility, pedestrian flow, or that presents other types of obstacles should be removed. But the removal should be by way of selective pruning or "thinning out." Such branch removal should be back to main lateral branches or to the trunk, not by nonselectively chopping the top off from all branches that stick up beyond a certain height.

Anyone who employs topping or advertises this service should be avoided. Too often these people take advantage of the ignorance of their customers, and see an easy way to make money by quick work with their chain saws. A trained arborist who understands tree growth would not condone tree topping except under unusual circumstances (e.g., clearance for power lines or possible damage to a building). Many cities have enacted ordinances that ban the topping of street trees.

Many people believe that all old trees should be topped to lengthen their life span, but age is not a justification for tree topping. Healthy limbs on old healthy trees should be left alone whenever possible. Topping creates stubs that disfigure trees, leave entry ports for disease and insect problems, and may give rise to a mass of vigorous, upright "water sprouts." Water sprouts are less structurally sound than regular branches, and actually regrow faster than normal growth, creating size and repruning problems more quickly.

Topping also creates other, more subtle problems. It removes plant tissue needed for food production — the tree's crown may be reduced via topping, but there is still a large root system that needs to be fed in order to keep the tree healthy. Topping removes tree leaf cover that shades the trunk and keeps it from scalding in direct sun and also removes buds that would form a "normal" branch system, especially on trees that produce few water sprouts.

If a tree is really old and unhealthy, or a hazard, it should be removed altogether. If a replacement is desired, corrective pruning should be started immediately and carried out on a yearly basis as needed. A little preventive care can save a tree from a topping death when the tree gets older. ∎

◀ These silver maples have been topped. Now they are not only weaker for lack of good and even branch growth, but also disfigured and unattractive.

▲ A close-up of one of the unsightly water sprouts found on the silver maples shown above. Water sprouts often develop when a tree is topped.

How Trunk Wounds Weaken or Kill Plants

When a lawn mower or any other piece of equipment hits a plant (whether accidentally or not) and strips away part of the bark, or puts a hole in the trunk, many people see little more than the cosmetic damage that has been inflicted. Appearance is important, but what is more crucial is the damage to both the tree's structure and its physiological processes.

Trees and other plants cannot heal wounds in the sense that animals and people can. Trees cannot generate new cells to replace cells that have been lost or damaged. Instead they respond to wounds by attempting to wall-off or compartmentalize them. The tree undergoes a process known as closure in which callus cells are produced that allow the tree to form actual physical boundary layers around the wound. These layers prevent insect and disease organisms, which may use the wounds as entry ports, from spreading into sound or healthy tissue.

A second process that starts when a wound is inflicted occurs internally. We do not normally see its results unless we actually cut into the plant. This second process or wound response is called compartmentalization, and is designed to limit any decay that may develop to the wounded area. Cells begin to

form a chemical barrier in four planes around a wounded area, physically walling the wounded area off from healthy tissue. If a tree compartmentalizes well it keeps decay from spreading into healthy tissue. The wounded area will stay permanently separated unless something breaks through one of the compartmentalization barrier walls. ▶

▲ A compartmentalized tree wound showing new growth around the wound boundary.

▲ The swollen ridge of tissue surrounding the wound is the callus tissue that tried to close the wound, which in this case, never completely happened.

◀ Basal (meaning situated at the base) tree wounds, such as the one shown here, can eventually lead to tree death.

How successful a tree is at compartmentalizing a wound depends on the species, age, health, and vigor of the tree. Some species are strong compartmentalizers and can recover from minor damage quite readily (green ash, sweet gum). Other species are weak compartmentalizers and can be easily killed if injured a few times (river birch, honey locust).

Even within one species of tree there will be individuals and clones that compartmentalize better than others. Considerable tree breeding and selection work is being carried on to be sure that future landscape trees will be better able to respond to wounds.

In addition to opening up entry ports for pests, wounds destroy structurally supportive cells and tissues that carry water and nutrients throughout the tree. Just beneath the bark are the cells (phloem) that carry nutrients manufactured (photosynthesized) by the leaves down to feed the roots.

If the phloem cells are injured or removed, less food will reach the root system, thus weakening it. A weakened root system will have a reduced ability to support the tree and to absorb the water and nutrients it needs. This will start the tree into a cycle of steady decline unless it can compartmentalize the wound readily and regain a healthy status via proper cultural practices.

Interior to the phloem is the cambial layer that yearly replaces and/or adds to the phloem and the cells interior to the cambium (xylem). Cambial cells are actively dividing cells that contribute to the increase in a tree trunk's diameter each year by adding a new layer or ring of xylem or wood.

This new layer contains cells through which water and nutrients move up from the roots to the leaves. One reason that a tree's leaves wilt when the trunk is wounded is because these "water pipes" are severed. Again, this type of wounding contributes to a cyclical weakening of the tree. The leaves that no longer are getting water and nutrients cannot manufacture food with which to feed the roots to aid in their continued uptake of additional water and nutrients.

Because tree trunk wounds are so debilitating, adequate remedial measures should be undertaken. If the bark has very recently been pulled away from the trunk it should immediately be pushed back against the trunk and held in place by wrapping or tying it securely.

If the wound occurred so long ago that the bark and wood tissues have dried, the cambium will not be able to "knit" the tissues back together. In this case the dead bark should be cut away back to moist, living tissue. A clean edge should be cut or "scribed" around the wound, cutting no further into healthy tissue than necessary. No special scribing need be fashioned as was once recommended, and no tree wound paint

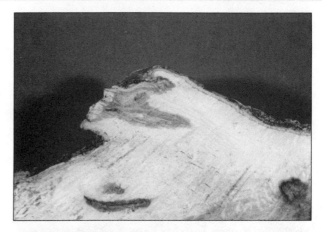

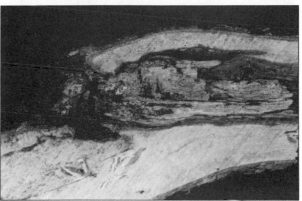

▲ The top photo shows good wound compartmentalization — there is a very limited column of decay because the branch bark collar was not removed. Bad wound compartmentalization (bottom) is characterized by an extensive column of decay, probably caused because both the branch and the branch bark collar (needed to aid the compartmentalization process) were removed.

or dressing should be applied.

After reattaching the bark or scribing the wound, the tree should be watered and fed to insure the vigorous growth that will aid the tree in its recovery, and all attempts should be made to insure that the tree will not be further injured.

Wound closure and compartmentalization occur not only when a plant is wounded, but also when a plant sheds parts, such as the dropping of an old bottom branch on a forest tree. Although we should exercise extreme care to avoid wounding our plants, once a wound occurs and a plant responds to it, we should avoid damaging its natural defense mechanisms through improper pruning or the unnecessary use of wound paint or sealants. ■

be discussed in later chapters, so for now here is a list of some of these contributing factors.

- Plants moved or transplanted at the wrong time of year or with the wrong root treatment.
- Trees and shrubs planted too deeply or too shallowly, or in too small a planting hole.
- Trees and shrubs planted with root-constricting containers or materials around their root balls.
- Trees and shrubs planted with excess backfill amendments such as peat moss and ground pine bark.
- Trees with tree wrap and staking left in place too long (Figures 4-4 and 4-5).
- Trees and shrubs with no mulch that serves to reduce weed competition and equipment damage and conserve soil moisture.
- Plants improperly treated with pesticides and fertilizers.
- Trees and shrubs improperly pruned (Figure 4-6).
- Plants inadequately watered.

This is by no means a complete list of planting and cultural mistakes, but it contains the major contributors to plant decline and shows the areas to which particular attention should be paid in order to improve the growth of your landscape plants.

Figure 4-7. A major branch was torn away from this tree by a strong wind; this area needs immediate attention if more severe damage (in the form of pests or diseases) is to be prevented.

CHANGES IN THE LANDSCAPE

Many plants in a landscape begin to decline due to physical changes in the site, or because of changes in the ways a family uses a landscape. An area that is used for many years as a path may become devoid of vegetation due to soil compaction. Flowering shrubs that once bloomed profusely in a sunny location may fail to bloom at all if an addition added to the house puts the shrubs into dense shade.

As with compaction, any other changes to the soil, such as elevation changes or changes in drainage patterns, can cause plants to decline. So too can the addition of other plants or of structures such as patios, pools, and storage buildings that may change how light falls or where it is reflected, where and how precipitation falls, or where winds blow. Not only will site and use changes on a

Figure 4-8. A good way to prevent, or lessen the effects of, landscape plant problems is by routine monitoring.

particular property affect the landscape plants there, so too will changes on adjoining properties, and in some cases, on properties further separated.

When a homeowner plans to make a change that could impact on the landscape, everything should be done to minimize injury to plants. Plants may need to be moved, pruned back, or in some cases even removed. When changes will be made on surrounding sites, little or no control over the results may be possible. If detrimental effects occur, undertake whatever can be done to minimize plant decline as a result of these changes. Since changes in physical characteristics and uses of a landscape are inevitable, everything should be done to keep each plant's microenvironment as close to what it requires as possible.

Damage Due to Weather or Disaster

From time to time some form of natural disaster will impact every landscape. It may be fires that burn plants, winds from hurricanes or tornadoes that uproot plants, ice loads from winter storms that break branches off, strikes from lightning that split tree trunks open, or waters from floods that suffocate roots. Although little can ever be done to prevent a natural occurrence, anticipate as much as possible in order to minimize potential damage to landscape plants. Weak branches can be pruned off and poorly rooted trees can be staked, but little more may be possible. Once natural disasters have occurred, quick action must be taken to correct the damage. Burned areas can be replanted, uprooted plants can be replanted or removed, broken branches can be properly pruned off, and saturated soil can be aerated.

Actually, more damage often occurs not because immediate repair measures are neglected, but because uncorrected damage can create entry ports for secondary pests, such as insects and decay fungi, that can do even more serious damage. The sooner damage from any cause is attended to, the less trauma the plants will eventually experience (Figure 4-7).

PESTS AND DISEASES

Many homeowners could very easily reduce the decline of their landscape plants if they would take a few minutes every other week from spring through fall to monitor their plants for insect and disease problems (Figure 4-8). These pest organisms cause the decline and death of many plants each year, and yet if their presence is detected before they have become widespread or inflicted much damage, many can easily be suppressed or eliminated.

By the time many homeowners realize there is a problem, the plants are often disfigured or too badly damaged to be saved. Often, too, even though a problem is recognized early on, the problem is misdiagnosed or treated with the wrong control measure (there is more on pest control in chapter 7).

Another difficulty is the fact that many people do not realize that the same symptoms a plant exhibits for certain insect and disease problems (such as wilt, leaf spots, dead leaf tips and margins, dead twigs) can instead be the symptoms of nonpathogenic, abiotic, or what are often referred to as physiological diseases. Physiological diseases are caused by nonliving, environmental, or cultural factors such as air pollution, compacted soil, or herbicide spray drift (Figure 4-9). Before a supposed insect or disease problem is treated as such, it is important to rule out a physiological problem.

In addition to insects and diseases that are living pest problems, there are other living organisms that can cause plant damage and decline, including large animals (e.g., deer and dogs) and rodents (e.g., rabbits, moles, mice, or voles). Frequently these animals leave not only symptoms (damaged bark, missing buds), but also signs such as tracks or droppings that help in their identification and formulation of a control measure.

DIMINISHED LIGHT, SPACE, AND WATER

As our planet becomes more populated and we feel the pressure and stress created by living with so many people, so too do plants feel population pressure and stress as they compete with surrounding plants for physical space, sunlight, water, nutrients, and other essential items that they must share.

Next time you're in a wooded area, notice that the bulk of the branches on all but the trees on the edges of the woods are at the top of the trunk. Below that top area you will find mainly stubs where branches have broken off. What you are seeing is a form of self-pruning that trees undergo when the amount of light reaching the interior of the tree canopies diminishes as more branches grow at the top of the tree. At some point, too little sunlight gets to the lower branches to keep their leaves manufacturing food, and rather than let these nonfood producing branches become a drain, the tree "prunes" them off.

Also, small seedlings often fail to become large trees in part due to the reduced light intensity under the larger trees and in part due to the space competition with the larger trees. This is one of the reasons that the majority of younger trees in a wooded location are seen on the edges or fringe of that area where space and light competition is less. This light-reduction phenomenon occurs in the landscape, too, as trees that once branched low to

Figure 4-9. This physiological problem could have had many causes, including hail, mechanical injury, or vandalism.

the ground loose lower branches, or shrubs that once were covered with flowers only have flowers on the upper and outer ends of branches.

Light and physical space aren't the only factors that plants compete for. They compete heavily for water and the dissolved nutrients contained in the water they absorb. Plants have various genetically controlled abilities to obtain, absorb, and retain water, those abilities being dependent on the type and extent of root system they form, the type of "interior plumbing" they contain for water movement, and the orientation and physical makeup of their leaves.

Because some plants will compete less effectively than others when space, sunlight, water, nutrients, and other important elements for growth are in limited supply, different plants will be able to survive better under different landscape conditions. For this reason we need to know, for example, which plants are more drought tolerant, so that when water is in short supply we can give our limited water to those plants that will suffer most from a shortage of moisture.

Either we must do the above preferential watering, or we need to begin planting our landscapes with more environmentally tolerant plants. The new concept of xeriscaping relates to this in that its principal goal is to use plants that require less water.

PLANT ABUSE

Landscape plants, trees in particular, are frequently wounded and vandalized. Not that most of us set out to maliciously harm our landscape plants, but all too often they are either there when we need something functional, or are in the way and become an obstacle.

When trees are used as posts to which we tie or attach things, the trunk is usually wounded in one of two ways. Sometimes the rope or wire we tie around the plant abrades or rubs through the bark and opens up a wound through which detrimental insect and disease organisms can enter. Sometimes we leave whatever we have tied around the tree in place for such a long period of time that as the tree trunk increases in diameter, the tying material cuts through or girdles the plant. The girdling action can then eventually kill the tree if it blocks food

Figure 4-10.   This tree has begun to grow over the bracket nailed to it. If the bracket were removed it would open up the wound area that the tree has compartmentalized.

from being translocated (transported) down from the leaves, through the bark, to the roots.

When trees are used to hang signs, we wound the trees by opening up holes to the interior wood as we bang nails and other attaching devices into the trunk. If the nails are left in place, the trees compartmentalize the wound areas around the nails (Figure 4-10). It is actually preferable to leave the nails in the trees and have natural wound barriers form around them than to keep pulling out and banging in new nails, each time opening up new wounds.

Trees are wounded by what we would consider vandalism when people carve their initials into the bark, or swing on and break off branches. Neither of these types of wounds may kill the tree, but they will nonetheless render the trees less aesthetically appealing, and may, as above, open up entry ports for insect and disease organisms.

One of the major ways in which trees get wounded is when they get in our way. How many people who mow the lawn can honestly say that they've never run into a tree trunk or hit a tree's trunk with a string weed trimmer? Damage from lawn-maintenance equipment is actually the number-one killer of our landscape trees (Figure 4-11). Add to that the people who run into trees, especially with their cars, and it's a wonder trees haven't evolved with legs by now so that when they see a person coming they can get out of the way!

Figure 4-11. The wound at the base of this tree is from a lawn mower or string trimmer. Mulch was applied too late to prevent such damage by maintenance equipment.

CHEMICAL DAMAGE

An unseen killer of landscape plants is the misuse of chemicals, again an area where few people are guilty of malicious intent. Just as we unknowingly damage a tree's trunk, we often damage not only the above-ground portions of landscape plants by the misuse of chemicals, but frequently the unseen, below-ground root systems that are critically important to plant health and vigor.

When it snows or the road or sidewalk becomes covered with ice, we try to make conditions safer by melting the ice or snow, frequently with a deicing chemical that is toxic to plants. Many salt compounds are used which can burn or desiccate not only leaves (by direct contact or spray drift), but also underground roots when the salts get washed into the soil. Salts can also cause the structure of the soil to break down so that it becomes less permeable to air and water.

Herbicides that are used to control weeds, or any other plants that we think of as undesirable, will also kill desirable plants if they are applied to, or allowed to drift onto, them. Always read the label of any herbicide product very carefully to be sure you are applying it to the right target weed, at the right time of year or stage of weed growth, at the right concentration, and with the right equipment. Be sure to exercise any precautions listed on the label, and check to see what landscape plants may also be damaged or killed. Trees and shrubs will generally tolerate herbicide misuse to a greater degree than small annual flowers, perennials, or ground cover plants, but why risk harming any nontarget plant?

Other pesticide misuse can be damaging. Though insecticides are designed to kill insects and not plants, often materials that act as carriers of the active ingredients can also damage plants if applied at too high a rate. And since pesticides such as fungicides and bactericides are working against organisms that are actually plants, they can damage the plants you want to protect for that reason or for the same reason that insecticides can cause damage.

Another material that normally enhances plant growth, but can also cause damage if misapplied, is inorganic fertilizers. The old adage that if a little is good, a lot is better, does not apply to inorganic fertilizer (ammonium nitrate, iron sulfate) use. Overapplication of fertilizers can very quickly kill (mainly by desiccation) the plants you were hoping to stimulate into healthy growth.

The family pet could be killing your favorite shrub. If male dogs urinate on certain species of shrubs the salts in their urine may burn the foliage. This is especially true with evergreen shrubs.

There are many other subtle, and often unseen chemical killers. Air pollutants and acid rain from factory and car emissions kill plants. Underground gas leaks and above-ground dumping of solvents, oils, and other chemicals kill plants. Materials disposed of by burial or burning can kill plants. You can individually exercise care with the use of chemicals around your own landscape plants, but there are many environmentally misused chemicals over which you will have no control that will damage your plants. To help prevent this misuse, always encourage the safe and proper use and disposal of all chemicals.

5

STEPS IN RENOVATION AND REDESIGN — ON PAPER

It's time to put all of the information that has been presented in the first four chapters to work by going out and actually surveying your landscape and putting your observations and measurements on paper. By thoroughly analyzing your own particular situation you will be able to custom-design a renovation plan and program to fit your needs at present and for the future.

CREATE A SCALE DRAWING

First, see if you have a survey plat (a scaled map showing actual or proposed features) of your property. If so, you can scale it up (draw it larger) so that you can put all of your analysis and observations on paper. If not, see if you can get a copy from your bank, builder, or someone else who might have a copy. If still unavailable, check with your city or county government to see what is recorded. If an actual plat isn't recorded, a legal description outlining the boundaries should be available.

If no scaled plat is available, buy or borrow a measuring tape at least 50 feet long, but preferably 100 feet long for a large property. Measure your property boundary using whatever markings or features you are sure of and consult the legal description. If part of what you record as your property is actually city easement, be sure to note that fact.

Next, measure the exterior dimensions of your house and how it is located on the property, then draw the house to scale on the property (Figure 5-1). Use a large enough scale (1 inch = 10 or 20 feet may be adequate) so that you have plenty of room on the paper to record both house and landscape details. It will be easier to draw to scale if you use a scale ruler or draw on graph paper where you can count squares for certain footages. Be sure to record the scale you are using (1 inch = 10 feet, 0 inches; 1 square = 2 feet; etc.).

Locate on the outline of your house all first-floor windows, noting how high they are off the ground, and all doors, showing the direction in which they swing or slide. Also note any other structural details that could impact your landscape design, such as roof overhangs or exterior basement entrances. Within the outline of the house, label how you use all first-floor rooms.

Next, locate where downspouts and outdoor faucets attach to the house, as well as electrical outlets and air-conditioning units. Show where

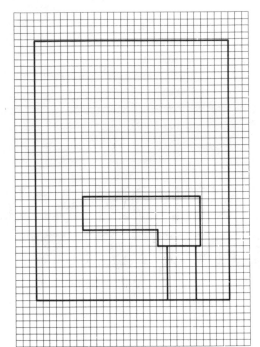

Figure 5-1. ◀ Draw your house on a piece of lined or graph paper and devise a scale that will be roughly equivalent to reality — this will then become your scale drawing from which all renovation and redesign can be done in advance of the actual work. Be sure to leave enough room on the drawing to later draw in features of your home and landscape on overlapping layers.

Figure 5-3. ▶ The master base plan is further enhanced by the addition of landscape features that may not be immediately apparent: how high have trees/plants grown; how do the properties abutting yours affect your landscape, if at all; what is the direction of prevailing winds, and how does the sun fall at different times of the year; are there any significant slopes or grades; and are there any views worth considering?

Figure 5-2. ▶ A "base plan" of your landscape, derived from the original scale drawing you did of the property, will be necessary before renovation work can begin. You may want to do a rough sketch first, then redraw it as neatly as possible to create a master base plan. It should show all the features of the site, home, and property: large landscape elements (big trees, a sizable hedge), where the roof and/or gutters drain; location of utility services (both above- and underground); permanent features such as driveways, paths, fences; and how rooms are used on the first floor of the house.

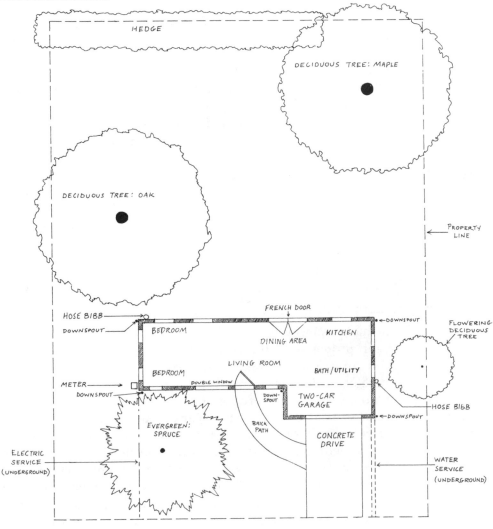

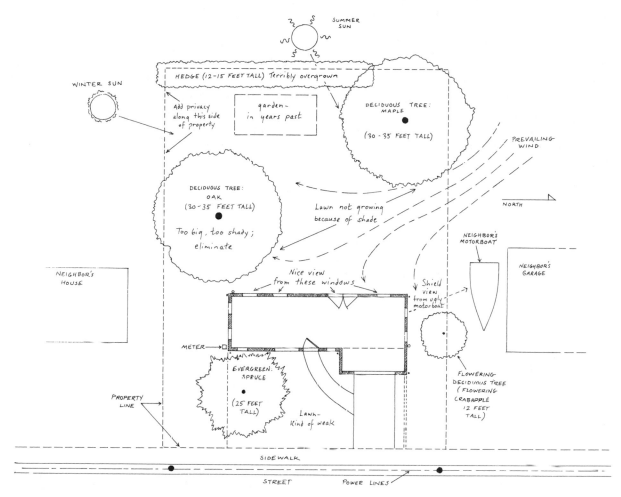

utilities enter the house, where they cross the property (above or below ground), and where any meters may be located (Figure 5-2). If you are in doubt where underground utilities (and items such as septic tanks and wells) are located (or how deep they are), call the utility companies and ask them to come flag the locations so that you won't mistakenly plant a new tree on top of a water line. Also find out from the utility companies, and record, the type of easements they may have (e.g., 10 feet around power lines).

Next, locate any sidewalks, driveways, paths, patios, decks, pools, detached garages, storage buildings, and other structures on your property that will definitely stay where they are presently located. Show any fences and walls, being especially careful to note any land between a fence or wall and a neighbor's property line. Do the same for less permanent structures or features such as above-ground movable pools, dog pens, clotheslines, children's play equipment, vegetable gardens, compost piles, and any other features that you probably will not relocate.

Now draw on your property/house plan or on two separate overlays the structural elements that will be changed and all existing vegetation regardless of status or condition. Show the actual spread of each plant, even if they overlap, and record the height of all trees and shrubs. Then note either on the plan, the overlay itself, in the margin, or on a list with codes or a legend, the approximate ages and conditions of all existing plants. Do not at this point make decisions as to what stays or gets moved or removed.

Next, label any other site details that could influence your renovation. Show existing slopes, prevailing wind directions, sun and shade patterns (you should put the compass points on your plan), and views onto and off from your property. Write around the outside of your property line any details on neighboring properties that could influence your decisions. Figure 5-3 is an example of how such a plan would look on a single sheet of paper (ie., without overlays).

Here is a summary of what you should put on your scale drawing.

Developing a Series of Overlays

If your property is large or heavily planted, or if there are many important site details that you should record, it may be helpful to develop a series of overlays in order not to force too much information on your original property plan.

A series of four overlays can be developed on paper that you can see through, such as tracing paper, thin drafting paper, or buff-colored design paper often referred to as dogtag. It will be easier to make notes and erasures on these sheets, or to throw these sheets away if major changes are needed, than to damage your original drawing.

You may want to draw only the property lines, house outline and details, permanent paving and structures, and utility locations on your original drawing. Then on one overlay draw all existing plant material, and on another draw various structural elements and all important on-and-off-site details if they are too numerous for the original drawing. As decisions are made regarding removing, moving, and renovating existing plants, these details can be shown on yet another overlay, perhaps color-coded by activity. This can serve as a work plan for the initial "clearing and rearranging" installation stage.

Once the above work has been completed, develop a final overlay showing all the new plants and improvements you are adding. This can serve as a work plan for the "new installation" stage. Use these four overlays freely to help in developing the renovation plan that will most closely fit your needs. The cost of a series of overlays will be minimal compared to investing in a landscape renovation. ∎

- Property lines, noting city easements.
- House location and its exterior outline.
- Placement of doors and windows on the first floor, noting height of windows aboveground, showing directions in which doors swing or slide, and noting any other important details.
- Label first-floor rooms in the house.
- Utility locations and where they attach to the house, and utility meters.
- Sidewalks, driveways, paths, patios, decks, detached garages, storage buildings, and other permanent structures; fences and walls, pools, dog pens, play areas, vegetable gardens, etc., that will not change in location.
- Note important site details such as slope, wind direction, and views. Do this also for bordering properties. Be sure to indicate compass directions.
- Draw in or note anything else that your analysis turns up which might have an impact on your renovation.
- You should also have on your plan or on your separate overlays: structural items and areas that can or will change, and all existing landscape plants with notes about their approximate ages and conditions.

You should now have before you a scale drawing of your property, house, and landscape with important notes about bordering properties and site details and possibly also some related overlays. These items will serve as the basis from which you can plan and draw a landscape renovation.

You may also find it helpful to take several pictures of your house and property, looking toward it from surrounding properties and looking out in the directions of major views. These pictures can be helpful to have as you sit and develop your renovation plan from your scale drawings and the needs analysis you will do next.

A QUALITATIVE ANALYSIS — NEEDS AND DESIRES

Now it is time to make an analysis different from the one made of the landscape and its plants. You should analyze what the members of the household need and want from the landscape at present, and what they may need and want from it in the future. Whereas landscapes once emphasized aesthetics or just visual appearance, the emphasis now is on how functional landscapes can be. Be realistic about the future and plan for as long a time as you may keep the house. Also keep in mind those landscape elements that may increase the salability of your house, if that prospect is in the not-too-distant future.

Your user analysis should include such things as gardening, recreational, and entertaining needs, along with utilitarian needs such as storage areas for extra vehicles, boats, trash cans, and firewood. As leisure time increases for many people, their landscape becomes a greater extension of their indoor living space, and sees ever-increasing use. The sample questionnaire on page 60 shows the kind of

Energy Conservation by Effective Landscaping

When designing your landscape renovation, keep in mind several things that can be done to conserve energy. Use plants that aesthetically enhance your property and can also serve to modify the environment in which you place them.

The following is a list of some of the major uses of plants for energy conservation.

- Plant large deciduous trees on the south, southwest, and west sides of houses, patios, decks, and outdoor recreation areas for summer shade.
- Plant deciduous vines on supports or trellises against walls on the south, southwest, and west sides to again provide summer shade. These vines can also have an insulating effect in winter.
- Plant evergreen or deciduous shrubs to shade all but the northern side of air-conditioning units.
- Plant evergreens close to your house on the northwest side (and/or northeast — depending on prevailing winds) to create a dead space and insulate against winter winds.
- Plant staggered, double rows (if space permits) of tall evergreen shrubs or trees on the northwest (or northeast) side of the house to block or divert the winter wind, and to control drifting snow.
- Plant tree and shrub groups to direct the wind in desirable directions, allowing cold air to settle downhill whenever possible.
- Plant trees and shrubs to intercept the light and heat bouncing up from light-colored paved surfaces. ∎

questions to ask to obtain a useful landscape analysis.

If you decide to add a pool, storage shed, patio, fence, or additional parking space, be sure to check what ordinances, regulations, or permits may be necessary. Also get dimensions that can be used on your renovation drawing so that space can be committed or readjusted for specific needs. More permanent features such as these should be planned and space allocated for before more flexible features such as play areas and vegetable gardens are designed.

Anticipate, as much as possible, every immediate and future use and need to avoid having to add something at a later time that may disrupt the organization and flow of your design. Adding unplanned items is what obliges many people to redo their landscapes as structures and plants fail to coordinate.

Combine as many use areas as possible, such as a combination trash can/firewood storage area, or an additional parking area that can also service as a sports area. Space is more and more at a premium in most landscapes, and even if it is not, there is no need to commit more space to paving and structural use than necessary. Utilitarian areas can be expensive to develop and eat up land that could be better used for vegetation, which is becoming so scarce in some parts of the country. Be realistic about what you might want and what you will be able to afford, both in purchase or installation costs, and in future maintenance time and expense.

From the above analysis develop a list ranked by priority and realistic affordability. Also indicate how soon you would like to add these features. Now take this list and begin to rough out on an overlay of your scaled drawing where these areas or items can go. In doing this drawing you may find it helpful to draw several overlays or plans showing alternative ways to commit the space you have available. Look for easy flow or transition from one area to the other (Figure 5-4). If you have to walk through the dog run to get to the swimming pool or children's play area, you may quickly find this to be unacceptable.

Areas in the landscape were once delineated as belonging to the public, private, or service area. The public area was the area visible in front of the house and from the street. The private area was the area that the occupants used at their discretion, the service area was the area whose purpose was utilitarian.

Although the landscape can still be divided into these three use areas, there is frequently overlap in usage, and therefore it is probably easier just to outline what is needed and find appropriate areas. Whenever possible, however, the public area should be kept simple and attractive with utilitarian and private functions reserved for less visible areas (Figure 5-5).

DEVELOPING A FINAL PLAN

You now have as part of your renovation drawings a rough use-assignment plan showing where you want to add various items to your landscape.

Edible Landscaping

Most of our landscapes today are predominately ornamental and do not make use of the many edible plants that can also function as landscape plants. As you select plants for your landscape, consider using plants that provide food in addition to shade and beauty. Food plants often complement ornamental plants, and the combination can easily increase the value of your landscape.

The easiest place to start is by using fruit-bearing trees and shrubs as ornamentals. The flowers on many plants are as showy as those on related ornamentals, and the fruit they produce is then an added benefit.

In place of large shade trees there are fairly tall native fruit trees and a number of nut trees that can be used. Although using fruit and nut trees and shrubs may increase plant litter and maintenance chores, they can function very effectively in any landscape if pest-resistant varieties are used and if their locations are carefully selected.

The choices of edible plants is not limited to trees and shrubs. Many vines, in particular annual vines, bear edible parts, and many herbs or spreading plants such as strawberries can serve as ground cover substitutes in low-traffic areas. Many of the leafy vegetables and plants (asparagus, for example) can be interspersed amongst perennial and annual flowers. Keep in mind that when annuals die there will be voids left, so plan and locate these edible plantings accordingly, and be sure to use them in areas where they will be easy to maintain and harvest. ■

▲ A bed of strawberries was used as a ground cover here to eliminate the need to mow in the area where the lawn met the stone retaining wall.

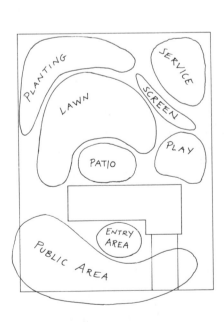

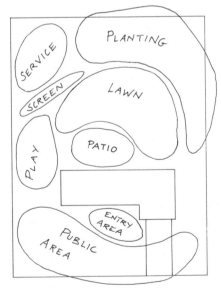

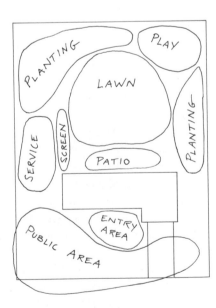

Figure 5-4. Three different goose-egg studies of the same landscape that show a variety of ways in which the space can be used. This is a valuable way to evaluate how you presently use, and propose to use, the landscape after a renovation has been completed.

You now need to compare this use plan with your existing landscape in order to decide how to rearrange the existing landscape to accommodate the new needs and wants.

Take the overlay or plan on which you have indicated all existing plants, and decide and indicate what plants are definitely being removed and disposed of based on the information gained from chapters 2 and 3. Do that also with the plan or overlay showing any structures or paving that can be moved or removed. This can now serve as a guide for work that can be started while you are developing a final plan.

Next develop a plan or overlay that shows what of the existing landscape you hope to maintain (even if renewal pruning is needed), and what you would like to use if it can be moved to an appropriate location. As mentioned earlier, do not, in your desire to save existing plants, impose any compromises on your design that may prove to be unsatisfactory in the future just for the sake of saving a plant or two.

Again as mentioned earlier, never assume that just because an area was once planted it should be replanted. When in doubt leave an area unplanted for several months, and then decide if a replace-

Figure 5-5. A vegetable garden is not appropriate in the front entry area of a house.

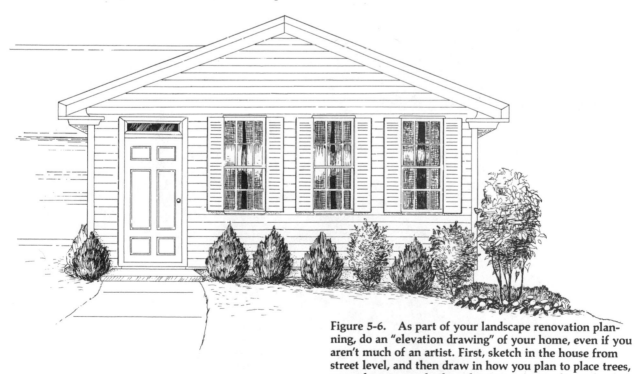

Figure 5-6. As part of your landscape renovation planning, do an "elevation drawing" of your home, even if you aren't much of an artist. First, sketch in the house from street level, and then draw in how you plan to place trees, ground covers, and other plantings as part of your landscape renovation. In the drawing above, the renovation will replace a monotonous row of evergreen shrubs with a variety of flowering evergreens and an interesting planting at the corner.

Figure 5-7. Slow-growing or dwarf cultivars of plants will reduce maintenance. Shown here are dwarf mugo pines.

Figure 5-8. Shrubs planted randomly, with no specific design and no unified bed, are harder to maintain and create a visual distraction (above). Plants grouped in mulched beds, on the other hand, are easier to maintain (right).

ment is really necessary. Also consider what type of plant to replant if you do decide something is needed in an area. Trees may be the most expensive to buy initially, but may be the least expensive to maintain in the long run. Conversely, a lawn may be the least expensive to initially install (if just quickly seeded in), but may be the most expensive to maintain once planted.

Compare this "to-stay" plan with the sketches you have done of a "future" landscape plan. Make any adjustments that are necessary to fit the two plans together, and then draw a final plan or overlay that shows to scale the final landscape with all plants and structures in their final locations. From this, a second work plan can be developed which shows plants and items that need to be moved. You may even want to do a sketch or elevation drawing of the front of your landscape to get an idea how the new landscape will look against or around the house (Figure 5-6).

As you develop your final landscape plan keep in mind the following items that can help to decrease future maintenance.

- Select low-maintenance plants — those with slow to moderate growth rates, high insect and disease resistance or tolerance, and no major cultural needs (frequent feeding, pruning) or litter problems (Figure 5-7).
- Carefully coordinate plant selection with the environmental conditions in which they will grow. Use native plants whenever possible and appropriate.

- Correct drainage and compaction problems before installing new plants.
- Select plants that can be pruned according to their natural form rather than in a stiff formal form.
- Install plants in groups in well-outlined, mulched beds rather than as solitary placements in the middle of lawn areas (Figure 5-8).
- Use curved and flowing lines for planting areas rather than sharp corners that can be difficult to mow around (Figure 5-9).
- Use ground covers and mulched areas in place of lawn to decrease mowing maintenance (Figure 5-10).
- Install irrigation systems wherever possible to provide regular watering in an easier and more efficient way.
- Use perennial plants in place of annual plants, or use a combination of annuals and perennials in flower beds.
- To obtain screening or privacy use structural materials (walls, fencing) in place of, or in combination with, plant material to decrease the maintenance of total plant material screens (Figure 5-11).
- Use high quality construction materials and plants.
- To reduce lawn wear and compaction problems, install permanent paving, wherever paths have worn (or where they may develop).
- Install pads for, or mulch under, items such as seats, tables, and trash cans to ease lawn maintenance around these areas.

Selection of New Plants

At this point no specific plants should be named on your plan other than those that are already in the landscape. The selection of actual new plants to add to your landscape should be a process in reverse. First a functional area is designed, and then an amount of permissible maintenance is assigned. After that, the types of plants with specific characteristics that will suit those areas are designated (e.g., a spring-flowering tree with a maximum height of 25 feet, spreading ground cover that tolerates light foot traffic, evergreen shrub for background that can be maintained in natural form to 3 feet), and then actual plants that fit those descriptions should be selected.

Make a list of plants with the various character-

Figure 5-9. Curved beds are easier to maintain and are more appealing visually.

Figure 5-10. Use mulched beds of ground covers (shown here are junipers) in place of lawn to reduce routine maintenance.

Figure 5-11. The privacy offered by a fence enclosure requires less maintenance than a plant screen or hedge.

Characteristics of Good Trees

Most landscape trees are used in one of three ways: as street trees, as shade trees, or as specimen trees. For each category there are different desirable characteristics that you should look for when selecting a tree. Characteristics of street trees should include:

- Hardiness and tolerance of urban conditions (e.g., dust, air pollution, vandalism, cultural neglect, compacted soil, drought).
- Low-maintenance requirements with no litter problems or hazards (e.g., thorns, poisonous fruit).
- Disease and insect resistance or tolerance.

- Straight trunks and high branching or branching that can be pruned up without destroying the trees' symmetry.
- Branches with wide crotch angles to minimize storm breakage or vandalism.
- Deep roots to prevent buckling sidewalks and interference with water lines.
- Long life (though most street trees "last" no more than ten to fifteen years).
- Not overly tall at maturity (especially if used under or near overhead power line).
- Crowns not so dense that light cannot penetrate to plant material growing underneath or to pavement that will need to dry after precipitation.
- Seasonal interest.

Shade trees should include the following desirable characteristics:

- Hardiness and low-maintenance requirements.
- Strong trunks and branches with a moderate growth rate.
- Long life.
- Crowns not so dense that they completely shade a patio or deck or that restrict light to plants growing underneath.
- Litter free if overhanging houses or paved structures. ▶

◀ **An example of a good street tree (Bradford pear).**

istics you prefer (mature height, maintenance requirements, flowering or evergreen), and compare that with lists of plants suitable to your environment. Such lists are available from your local Cooperative Extension Service and in references specific to your area. Visit garden centers, nurseries, parks, and other places that display plants to see what the plants look like before you make your final selection. Drive through neighborhoods to see how the plants look in actual landscapes.

If a suitable plant cannot be obtained locally, ask your garden center if they can order it for you or see if it is available from a mail-order nursery. Do not make compromises on plants that you really want until you have tried every available source.

ESTABLISH A TIME FRAME

At this point the various analytical and drawing components of your landscape renovation may have you a bit overwhelmed as to how to proceed. They may also have you wondering whether or not you can afford to renovate your landscape. The best thing to do now is to develop both a renovation calendar and a renovation budget and to proceed as time and money permit.

Chapter 6 will go into the actual execution of a renovation landscape plan in more detail, but the following is a summary of the activities involved:

▲ An example of a good shade tree (green ash).

- Flower colors that coordinate with surrounding plants and structures.
- Ability to attract wildlife.

Many times a tree must serve more than one function, such as providing shade and specimen interest, so select a tree with as many of the characteristics of both uses as possible. Of greatest importance (regardless of the tree's function) is the certainty that the tree is hardy enough for the area and suited for the microclimate in which it must grow. ■

For trees to be used as focal points or specimens in the landscape, the desirable characteristics include:

- Hardiness and low-maintenance requirements.
- Leaves, flowers, fruits, bark, and form provide multiseasonal interest.
- Litter is limited.
- Relative resistance to disease and insects.
- Ability to grow in location's microclimate.
- Self-pollinating capability (if possible) for fruit production.

▲ An example of a good specimen tree (pink flowering dogwood).

1. Remove plants that cannot be saved, rejuvenated, or moved.

2. Renovate or rejuvenate plants that will stay in place.

3. Move any existing plants that can be saved and used in other locations.

4. Install nonplant improvements such as paving, fencing, pools, and structures. This would also be the time to do any house renovation work such as adding a room or painting the exterior.

5. Select and install all new plants being added to the renovation plan.

6. Renovate the lawn and ground cover areas.

Add an estimated cost to each of the above. The first parts of the renovation calendar and budget are the least expensive parts up front — removing, rejuvenating, and/or moving existing plants. These activities should be undertaken first because they will then prepare the landscape for installation of new plants and features. They should also be a priority because waiting to remove, move, or prune plants and other items until after work has started may damage new plants or detract from new landscaping efforts.

If your budget is limited, this is all that you may be able to do initially, but it may surprise you to see how much better a landscape can look with nothing more than a few dead or declining plants removed and a few overgrown plants pruned back to

Understanding Plant Sizes

When you shop for plants at a retail nursery or garden center, you will find them in a variety of sizes and heights according to top growth (stems, trunks, and branches), and in a variety of packagings and ball sizes according to their roots. The American Association of Nurserymen publishes a document called the "American Standard for Nursery Stock." It is a set of guidelines for growers and wholesale nurseries that helps them standardize the sizing and descriptions of trees, shrubs, roses, bulbs, and other plant material. Though there is no law that requires adherence to these standards, the majority of growers follow the guidelines, thus there is relative uniformity in plant material, pricing and in marketing.

Using these standards, nursery professionals know what size root ball to dig for a small flowering tree, a tall coniferous tree, or a low spreading broadleaf evergreen shrub, for example. They know how to assign different grades to different qualities of plants, what they can use to wrap a field-dug root ball in, what the dimensions for various size containers should be, and other information that helps them produce and package a quality plant.

Trees are generally sold either by height (e.g., 3 feet to 4 feet, 6 feet to 8 feet) or by caliper (stem diameter measured at a certain height above the ground — ¾ inches, 1½ inches, 3 inches). Then, based on the height or caliper, the trees should have a root spread or root ball of a prescribed size (diameter and depth) whether they are bare-rooted, balled-and-burlapped, or container-grown.

Shrubs are generally sold wholesale by height (9 inches, 12 inches to 15 inches, 3 feet). For each height and shrub category (e.g., low-spreading evergreen, upright deciduous) there will be guidelines for spread, and in some cases, the number of stems or canes the shrub should have. When shrubs are container-grown they are generally sold by a combination of height and container size (1 gallon, 3 gallons).

■

▲ Shrubs, on the other hand, may be sold by container size. At left is a 3-gallon shrub, on the right is a 1-gallon shrub — both are shore junipers.

◄ Trees are often sold according to their caliper (stem or trunk diameter).

a natural, manageable size.

If the house is to be repainted, or an addition is planned, undertake such projects before finishing the landscape. Also install new paving, patios and decks, and sheds and storage buildings if possible before planting new plants or renovating the lawn.

If the installation of nonplant improvements must be prioritized, put improvements in the front of the property or in areas of greatest use or need at the top of the list. Do likewise with the addition of plant material. It is probably more important to plant a tree this year that can begin to grow and shade the house than to add a flower garden for enjoyment and cutting.

Always consider what will enhance the appearance of your property and increase its value. Use this approach whether you can afford to do the entire renovation job immediately, or whether it must be done over a period of time.

There are many ways to stretch a landscape budget, not only timewise as mentioned above, but also dollarwise. The following is a list of budget-stretching ideas to consider.

- Buy the smallest size plants that will still be effective. Smaller-sized trees and shrubs suffer from less root loss if field-dug, and therefore, begin to regrow at a faster rate than larger shrubs and trees. (Even consider buying small plants, potting them up into larger-sized con-

How Many Plants to Buy?

Even though you have roughed out areas on your plan drawing and overlays to plant or move new trees, shrubs, ground covers, and other plants, it is often hard to determine how many plants are actually needed. People often purchase and plant too many plants in an attempt to make a landscape look instantly "mature."

Start by finding out how large your desired plants will be in ten to fifteen years. If you want certain shrubs to always look like individual shrubs and not to merge into a planting mass, add a few feet to their eventual spread and use that as the space between centers. (If a shrub will spread to a 6-foot diameter, plant them 7 feet apart.) If you want the shrubs to merge into a hedge or screen, plant them closer than their maximum spread. The closer you plant them, the faster they will form a solid barrier, but also the faster your maintenance chores may increase. Consider the following calculations.

One hundred (100) plants spaced:

4 inches apart will cover 11 square feet
6 inches apart will cover 25 square feet
8 inches apart will cover 44 square feet
10 inches apart will cover 70 square feet
12 inches apart will cover 100 square feet
18 inches apart will cover 225 square feet
24 inches apart will cover 400 square feet

When trying to determine how many ground cover plants, annuals, or perennials to buy for an area, measure the area and calculate the number of square feet (1 foot x 1 foot = 1 square foot). Then, if you want to space the plants 1 foot apart, divide the total planting area's square footage by one to yield the number of plants you will need.

If the 1-foot spacing is too close for the eventual spread of the plants, or if they are too expensive to space that closely, increase the planting distance. If you put them on 2-foot centers (2 feet apart in a row and 2 feet between rows), each plant will be given or will cover 4 square feet. Divide the total planting area square footage by four to get the number of plants to buy.

These calculations will work whether the area is circular, square, or rectangular. When you install the plants be sure to offset rows by half the center distance so that plants are staggered in placement. Staggered placement gives faster coverage of an area and prevents a planting from looking like formal rows in both directions. It can also help prevent rain gullies (that encourage soil erosion) from forming between rows of plants.

Use the mature size of plants not only in determining how many plants to buy, but in deciding how to place them. If a tree will have a crown diameter of 30 feet, and you do not want it to touch or overhang the house, plant it at least 20 feet from the house. If a shrub you select will have an eventual spread of 6 feet but you only have a 4-foot wide planting strip between the house and sidewalk, realize that you will either need to constantly prune the plant to keep it in bounds, select a smaller plant, or you may need to move the walk, if you can, and widen the planting area. Architects frequently leave too small a space between houses and paving for planting. ■

---

tainers and feeding and watering them heavily for a growing season to force some fast growth before planting them in your landscape.)

- For deciduous trees and shrubs, buy bare-rooted rather than balled-and-burlapped (B & B) or container-grown plants whenever possible.
- Use fast-growing plants for short-term effects, or as substitutes, while slower-growing plants are getting established.
- Use smaller- or lesser-grade roses and bulbs and encourage rapid growth with good cultural practices.
- Use proven standard cultivars and varieties rather than new cultivars or introductions that are more expensive or that may not have been thoroughly tested in your area.
- Use inexpensive, fast-growing deciduous shrubs

in place of fencing or walls for a less expensive screen.
- Fit your design to the existing topography rather than attempting extensive regrading.
- When renovating the lawn, seed or sprig it (a small piece of grass stem and leaves) rather than sodding it.
- Construction materials that are larger (concrete blocks) are often less expensive than smaller units (brick).
- Propagate your own plants whenever possible.
- Use pavers or mulch for secondary walks rather than pouring solid surfaces.
- Use annual flowers as fillers while perennials and small shrubs develop good growth.
- Use more common, less expensive plants as backgrounds for more expensive, more notice-

Family Landscape Questionnaire

Family members

Name	Age	Sex	Special needs/interests
_____	_____	_____	_____
_____	_____	_____	_____
_____	_____	_____	_____
_____	_____	_____	_____

PERMANENT LANDSCAPE FEATURES

Identify those landscape elements that are permanent, such as paths, swimming pools, outbuildings, fences, etc. — the things around which a new/improved landscape will have to be designed. _____
_____
_____
_____

PUBLIC AREAS

Adequate space; more needed? _____ No. of cars _____
Driveway: does it provide enough parking? _____
Off-street parking? Enough for guests? _____
Are walkways, lighting, privacy satisfactory? _____

OUTDOOR LIVING AREAS

Is it presently   minimum maintenance ☐   moderate maintenance ☐   high maintenance ☐
What type of garden(s) do you have?:   ☐ flower garden   ☐ herb garden   ☐ vines
   ☐ fruit trees or bushes   ☐ vegetable garden   ☐ container garden   ☐ hobby garden
What are your favorite plants? _____
_____

Do you have a terrace, patio, or deck? Is it adequate to the needs of your family and guests (i.e., does it need more shade; is it convenient, comfortable)? _____
_____

What do you have in these sitting/eating areas (benches, tables, chairs, etc.)? _____
_____

Do you have a grill or barbecue; is it portable or permanent? How much do you use it? _____
_____

RECREATION AREAS

Is the lawn/play area adequate for all members of the family? What changes would you make? _____
_____

What use does this area get (kids' play space, badminton, croquet, horseshoes, etc.)? _____
_____

UTILITY/SERVICE AREAS   Do you have any of the following:

☐ compost/mulch pile   ☐ greenhouse/cold frame   ☐ trash storage
☐ dog house/dog run   ☐ other pets   ☐ clothesline (feet?) _____
☐ wood storage   ☐ storage of lawn and garden equipment
☐ storage of recreational vehicles (snowmobiles, boats, etc.)
Any changes needed/wanted in the utility/service areas? _____
_____

SPECIAL

Does your landscape attract wildlife (birds, other critters); do you want it to continue? _____
Do you have, or want to add, outdoor lighting, sculpture, a pond? _____

MAINTENANCE

What type of maintenance routine do you desire for your new landscape (i.e., less trimming, more mowing; a lot less mowing; less pruning; less work in general)? _____

able specimen plants.

- Use sand, gravel, or mulch as a construction base or pad rather than concrete.
- Recycle plants from the landscapes of neighbors.
- You can take a chance on "bargains" for easy-to-grow plants, and increase the plants' chances of survival with good cultural techniques.
- Buy plants in the fall when nurseries are clearing stock and offering lower prices.
- Install the less expensive plants first so that an area will look planted even if it is not complete.
- Compare prices and wait for sales — plants, like any other consumer goods, are subject to specials and sales.
- Space annuals, perennials, and ground covers further apart and use larger mulched areas in between.

Whenever possible, try not to sacrifice quality for price. Landscape as money allows and use smaller, good quality plants that are more likely to grow than larger, cheaper plants that may have been poorly treated and that will be less likely to reestablish successfully. And try to plan carefully so as to minimize the need to replant anything.

6

EXECUTING A LANDSCAPE RENOVATION

For many homeowners the process of scrutinizing their existing landscape and drawing a renovation plan is an exciting challenge that allows them to think analytically and use their artistic abilities. For others the exciting part is the stage in landscape renovation that we have now reached — working in the landscape, pruning shrubs, planting trees, and actually seeing the paper drawing take life.

REMOVAL OF EXISTING PLANTS AND SHRUBS

The first step in a landscape renovation involves removing existing plants that cannot be saved by spraying, pruning, or relocation (Figure 6-1). Removing plants may sound like an easy job, but it can be very difficult depending on the size of the plant, and even the type of foliage or stem modifications it has (e.g., thorns, spines). If small shrubs or trees are to be removed, all that may be necessary is to cut the tree trunk or shrub branches off as close to the ground as possible. Many plants will not sprout any new growth, and throwing a shovel of soil over any exposed stems will help to speed the rotting or decomposition of the roots.

The partial removal work mentioned above will be adequate if no replacement plants are to be installed in the same area, but if new trees and shrubs will be planted it is best to remove both the above-ground plant and as much of the root system as possible.

Before cutting and digging out plants, do whatever will be necessary to prevent damage to neighboring plants that are to be saved. Tie branches of trees and shrubs together or up out of the way to avoid damaging them, or put some form of barrier around them (Figure 6-2). For small shrubs and other low plants, such as perennials and ground covers, it may be easy to turn a bushel basket or trash can upside down over them to protect them. Be sure to separate plants that have intermingled so that you don't accidentally remove part of a plant to be saved as you cut and dig out a plant to be removed.

Keep in mind that as you dig out the root system of one plant you may be injuring or digging out portions of neighboring root systems as well. Concentrate on removing major roots that were located directly beneath a plant to avoid injuring the roots of others. Whenever possible, get a good grip on the roots and dig them out.

If the removal involves a large tree, for safety

Figure 6-1. These shrubs are overgrown and unattractive. They should be removed before new planting occurs.

Figure 6-2. Plant branches should be tied together, like the tree on the left, to minimize damage during the digging process.

reasons it is advisable to have an experienced, insured arborist do the work. Though the cost per tree may seem high, consider the expense if you are injured or your house damaged should you insist on doing it yourself. Often the price per tree is less if several trees are removed at one time. If you only have one tree that needs to be removed, see if neighbors have any that could also be cut down.

Whenever possible, salvage a healthy, cut tree for firewood (the wood must be seasoned first). If you don't have a fireplace or wood stove, try selling the wood to neighbors. Perhaps the tree service sells wood, and perhaps you can obtain a reduced price in exchange for the wood they obtain on your property. You also may be able to use their chipper or shredder to obtain a supply of "free" wood mulch from the smaller branches and debris.

RENEW EXISTING LANDSCAPE ELEMENTS

If instead of removing some of the plants from your existing landscape you hope to renovate and keep them, there are several things you may need to do. The most obvious chore will be to prune overgrown trees and shrubs. If you aren't familiar with how to prune a particular plant, consult one of the many good reference books or extension publications on the subject, or hire someone who has pruning experience to do the job for you.

Keep in mind that when pruning some plants, the time of year is crucial. If retention of flowers is important to you, and the plants are spring-blooming, any renovation or renewal pruning should be done after they flower in the spring and before they set their next year's buds in the fall. If the plants are summer-blooming, they can be pruned any time after they stop flowering in the summer until their new growth begins to set buds the following spring. For plants with inconspicuous (nonshowy) flowers, pruning can generally be done whenever it's necessary.

It will be easier to prune deciduous trees and shrubs when they are without leaves, usually from late fall until early spring (Figure 6-3). This will allow you to fully evaluate the crown of the plant to determine what should be removed. With evergreens there is no such "nonleaf" time, therefore they can be pruned at any point, although early fall pruning might stimulate new growth that could be killed if it has not become hardened prior to the first freeze.

Many deciduous shrubs can be totally renewed by cutting them off at ground level and allowing a whole new crown to develop from buds on the root system. This is generally not the case for evergreens, and the severity of pruning they can sustain varies widely. A good reference should be consulted before severely pruning back any plant.

Many plants can be "renewal pruned" if you feel that completely removing all top growth is too severe (even though a satisfactory new shrub can grow back in a year or two). With renewal pruning one-half or one-third of the shrub's stems are pruned back to the ground over two or three years until all of the old stems have been removed and replaced by new growth (Figure 6-4). This is a way to develop an entirely new crown in a couple of years without leaving an obvious hole at the beginning. (Again, this practice is primarily restricted to deciduous shrubs.)

The types of renovation and renewal pruning that will help to correct an overgrown shrub are generally too drastic for either deciduous or evergreen trees. Few trees can be cut off at ground level and adequately rejuvenated. Corrective tree pruning should concentrate on removing dead, broken, or crossing branches, and correcting narrow crotch angles (Figure 6-5).

If the height of a tree must be reduced, do not top the tree (see chapter 4). Remove branches that are too long back to the main branches or to the tree's trunk. If the tree has a main or central leader (giving the tree a pyramidal shape, as with many evergreen trees) there really is no way to cut back the tree's height without radically altering the shape of the tree's crown.

If ground covers and perennials need renovation, it is generally a matter of either pruning them back (or even mowing over them in the case of some ground covers), or digging, separating, and replanting them at new spacings. For many perennials there is a preferred time of year to dig and separate them, so be sure to consult a good reference on ground covers or perennials before reworking them.

Pruning isn't the only way to renovate plants that are to be retained. Plants may need to be treated for disease and insect problems, or be fed to

Figure 6-3. Deciduous plants are easier to prune when they are dormant and have no leaves masking their outline or branches.

Figure 6-4. Remove the oldest stems first, down to the ground in the manner shown above, when you renewal prune a shrub.

Figure 6-5. Corrective pruning of this tree would involve removing one of the branches that form this narrow crotch angle. But such pruning should have been done when the tree was much younger (and smaller).

restore more vigorous growth. They may also need to be weeded and mulched, and put on a more even watering regime. Adapting proper cultural practices will help to renovate or rejuvenate many plants whether or not they have outgrown their location and need pruning.

RENOVATING OR ADDING PERMANENT ELEMENTS

When people undertake a renovation of their landscape, they often forget to include nonplant elements in the landscape that may also need renovation or changing. Such items as walks, driveways, retaining walls, and privacy fences are an integral part of any home landscape.

Assuming that you have followed the steps in chapter 5 for designing and drawing a renovation plan, you will have included such nonplant items, but you need to think about what is the best time during the renovation process to attend to them. Because these items generally require some amount of construction, and perhaps large equipment, it is important to make nonplant renovations — additions, removals, or changes — at a point where damage will not be done to plants that

Figure 6-6. The concrete walk shown leads only to a busy street where no one can park or walk, and should be removed or redirected as part of a landscape renovation.

Figure 6-7. One way to develop a landscape elevation change is by constructing a berm, such as the one shown.

are being retained, moved, or added to the landscape.

After plants that are no longer functional have been removed, and after or while plants that are to be retained but that need some renovation or rejuvenation are being worked on, it is time to make nonplant alterations. Paving, decking, and other nonplant ground coverings should be removed or added, as should such vertical elements as walls and fences (Figure 6-6). If major structural items such as pools or gazebos are to be added, this is the time to do so.

If any changes in grade need to be made, do them at this time. Keep in mind that changing the soil level more than an inch or two around most trees and shrubs can kill them. If a change in elevation is desired, add a berm (a low mound of soil) or dig a low area as far away from planted areas as possible (Figure 6-7). If plants are small, dig and hold them for replanting once the grade changes have been made.

If low areas exist that do not drain well, or if planting areas frequently have standing water after heavy rains, consider regrading or installing drain tiles underground to help drain away extra water. In addition, be sure to install new underground water or electric lines while the ground is torn up for planting.

The major point here is to make such nonplant changes before the installation of new plants and the renovation of plant ground covers, in order to reduce the possibility of damaging any plant material. Care should naturally be taken to avoid damage to those plants that will remain in place.

Figure 6-8. Dormancy is over when plant buds begin to swell and break.

Figure 6-9. With the exception of small seedlings, evergreens should always be moved with a ball of soil — never bare-rooted.

Figure 6-10. With some advance planning, you can more successfully move a plant by root pruning it. Root pruning involves digging a narrow trench around the roots or breaking through the soil to outline the roots. New roots will form within the defined area and this will become the soil ball that will be moved with the plant.

SUCCESSFUL TRANSPLANTING

The two most critical factors in successfully moving plants are to move the plants at the right time of year relative to their growth cycles, and to dig and take as much of their root systems as possible.

Generally the best time of year to move plants is while they are dormant, a period of time when internal metabolic or physiological processes are at a minimum and virtually no external growth is occurring. This time period may vary from several months between midfall and early spring in northern areas, to a month or so in late winter in the South. In the deep South plants may never go into true dormancy, but may be more successfully moved when they are in a resting stage, a time when no new growth is being produced.

For deciduous trees and shrubs, dormancy is generally well established when their leaves are shed in the fall (Figure 6-8). The best time to move such plants will be between this fall leaf-drop period and when buds break and active growth resumes again in spring. Root growth in the soil continues long after the above-ground portion of the plant has ceased growing, and generally does not stop until the temperature of the soil falls below 40°F. Frozen ground is the major obstacle to moving plants during the dormant period.

There are some exceptions to the above generalization. Certain species of trees and shrubs do not transplant or move as well in the fall and winter as they do in the spring when growth is resuming. Again, check with the Cooperative Extension Service, your local garden center, or in a reference book about the particular plants you want to move to see if any fit this category.

Needle and broadleaf evergreens do not indicate dormancy to us visually by dropping their leaves in the fall. Evergreens will only drop all of their needles under severe conditions, such as summer drought or extreme winter desiccation. It is safe to assume that once the deciduous plants have dropped their leaves, however, the evergreens are also fairly dormant. Their dormancy period is generally a bit shorter than that of deciduous plants, though. Again, with a few exceptions, all evergreens should be moved before the deciduous plants break bud if at all possible.

Plants of all kinds can be moved at other times of the year if necessary. The key to successfully moving them while they are actively growing is to minimize transplant stress, which can be done by keeping them well watered and sheltered from the hot sun and drying winds until their roots have been reestablished.

As mentioned above, the second major factor in successfully moving plants involves digging as much of the plants' root systems as possible. Thus, the easiest plants to move and successfully replant will be relatively small deciduous trees and shrubs. They can often be dug and moved bare-rooted while they are dormant. At any other time, a ball of soil should be dug with their roots.

With large trees and shrubs, and with all evergreens, a ball of soil that surrounds the roots should always be dug (Figure 6-9). Evergreens in particular should never be moved bare-rooted. Evergreens always have leaves present that can begin to transpire (lose) water, and with a disturbed root system they will be unable to absorb water from the soil to keep the plant from drying out until new roots have regenerated.

If you can anticipate far enough in advance which plants will be moved, it helps to "root prune" them at least several months prior to their move. Root pruning involves digging a narrow trench or breaking through the root system with a spade or shovel, outlining the root ball to be moved with the plant (Figure 6-10). This practice will help to regenerate more roots within that root ball, so that a more extensive root system will be moved with the plant. Outline as large a root ball as possible, but remember that soil is heavy. For large plants that are of value, it may be necessary to have a piece of heavy equipment (tree spade, backhoe) come in and dig the plant.

Whether plants are dug bare-rooted or with a soil ball for moving, replant them as quickly as possible. Dig the planting holes at the new plant locations prior to digging up the plants to be moved, so that they can simply be taken from one location to the other and immediately replanted. Protect bare roots by covering them with a moist cloth or layers of moist newspaper.

When a soil ball is dug, something should be slipped under and around the ball, if possible, to wrap the ball tight before moving it (Figure 6-11). Keep the soil ball moist, which will prevent it from falling apart. Dry soil should be watered before a soil ball is dug.

If plants cannot immediately be replanted, their root systems must be protected from drying out as

Figure 6-11. When a plant is being moved, its soil/root ball should be wrapped securely to prevent breakage.

Figure 6-12. Plants offered for sale at garden centers or nurseries should be grouped by species and labeled with both Latin and common names. Descriptive information and general cultural requirements should also be provided.

Figure 6-13. Balled-and-burlapped (B & B) plants should have a root ball of adequate size relative to the plant, it should be well wrapped, and undamaged, as shown in the top photo. If the root ball looks like it has been rewrapped, dropped, or damaged (as shown in the bottom photo), don't buy the plant unless you can get a good guarantee.

described above. Protect soil root balls by either firmly wrapping them and tying or pinning the wrapping together, or if you have a container large enough, putting the root ball gently into a container. Keep the plants shaded and out of the wind until they can be replanted.

In addition to root pruning, pruning the top of the plant may be desirable prior to planting. Remove any broken or dying branches, do any corrective pruning that is needed, and if size reduction is desired, prune the plants back in their natural form as described in chapter 7. Do not simply take the hedge shears and chop the top of the plant back without regard to its natural form. Pruning prior to transplanting will reduce the moisture stress put on the leaves, but do not prune unless it is really needed.

Smaller landscape plants, such as ground covers and perennials, are less difficult to transplant because proportionately more of their roots can be dug and moved with them. Again consult a reference about the perennials you want to move because for many there are preferred times to dig, prune, and/or separate them. As with trees and shrubs, transplanting is generally more successful if a quantity of soil can be moved with the roots.

To replant the items you are moving, follow the correct planting procedures that are outlined on pages 68–70, which deal with how to properly install new plants into your landscape renovation.

JUDGING QUALITY

When you are ready to buy new plants, buy good quality specimens from reputable sources. It is possible to buy inexpensive plants, but be sure to distinguish between inexpensive and cheap ones. Mail-order nurseries can be a source for less expensive plants, but these plants will often be quite small, may get damaged during shipping, and may be inferior to what was pictured or claimed in the advertising.

Mass merchandisers, discount stores, grocery stores, and other outlets also generally offer plants with lower prices than retail garden centers and nurseries. There are trade-offs here as well, including less of a selection in terms of species and size, and often lower-quality plants (because they are inexpensive to produce and sell) that end up being fast-growing and/or short-lived.

Shopping for Plants by Mail

Many consumers are turning to mail-order buying these days because it is often more convenient and saves time. For gardeners it is also a way to increase sources of new, different, or unique items, particularly seeds, plants, gardening supplies, furniture, and landscape ornaments.

If you decide to do your garden shopping by mail, consider the following list of suggestions.

- First and foremost, buy from reputable firms. Ask gardening friends which companies they purchase from, look for the Mailorder Association of Nurseryman (MAN) logo in catalogs, or send for one of the prepared lists of mail-order sources that are often advertised in gardening magazines.
- Read all catalog descriptions carefully. Be sure tools and chemicals will do what you want. Be sure seeds and plants have the characteristics you desire — flower color, height and spread, time of bloom, hardiness, drought, and insect/disease resistance or tolerance. If claims sound too fantastic or prices seem too low, they probably are, and you'll get exactly what you pay for.
- Be sure there is a guarantee policy, and check to see what you must keep to use it — a copy of your order or a cancelled check. It is always a good idea to keep a copy of your order for your records.
- Pay particular attention to catalog numbers, quantities, substitution statements (whether or not you will accept a substitute), and prices. Have the items delivered to your place of employment if it is easier, or if you order plants that could be damaged by being left out in the cold, wind, or heat. If you require a specific delivery date, be sure to state that.
- Order early to avoid receiving a sold-out notice or an undesired substitute. This is especially true for new varieties of plants that may be available in only limited quantity.
- When your order arrives, unpack it immediately and check to see that it is complete and that all the plants are labeled. If items are missing, check for a statement explaining the omission (often it deals with plants being shipped according to their proper planting times). If no explanation is enclosed, contact the supplier immediately. If orders are damaged or plants are in poor condition, also make immediate contact.
- Store all products as directed, and install plants as soon as possible. If planting must be delayed, either temporarily heel plants in (place them in a transitional outdoor bed), or check roots for moisture, and moisten and repackage if necessary. Store plants to be held in a cool, dark location. If the plants are small, refrigerate them until planting is possible. If adequate planting directions have not been provided, request them.

Mail-order shopping for plants and supplies can be a rewarding experience, but remember, buyer beware! When you are dissatisfied, be sure to let someone know. ■

▶ **When your nursery mail order arrives, be sure that all plants are properly labeled so that you will know exactly what they are when it comes time to decide where and how to plant them.**

43425 Hosta Grandiflora

Also keep in mind that those retailers who offer less-expensive plants rarely offer any information on design, planting, or plant care. A bargain plant can become expensive if it dies and/or must be replaced frequently. Your money would have been better invested in the more expensive, better-quality or better-adapted plant in the first place, if some advice went along with the purchase.

If you are serious about your plant purchases, buy from a reputable garden center or retail nursery, ask friends and neighbors where they've made good purchases, or use the following points to determine for yourself whether you've found a good place to buy plants.

- The plants should look healthy, with leaves of proper size and color, buds that are plump and firm, and adequate numbers of flowers and/or fruits on those that are specimen ornamentals.
- The plants should be free of insects and disease signs or symptoms (e.g., spotted leaves, cankers on twigs), and there should be no weeds growing in the pots.
- The plants should be grouped by size and spe-

Figure 6-14. Before you buy container-grown or containerized plants, it is advisable to carefully remove the container to inspect root growth. The top photo shows acceptable root growth: an abundance of healthy, and usually white, root tips. If you find thicker roots circling around the outside of the container (bottom), chances are the plant is root-bound and could die from a main root girdling the stem no matter how well you care for it.

cies, with labels giving the plant's common and Latin (scientific) name, landscape characteristics, environmental requirements, and mature size, in addition to the price (Figure 6-12).

- Bare-rooted plants should have enough field roots from which new roots (important for absorbing water and nutrients, and anchoring the plant in the ground) will be able to regenerate.
- The root balls of balled-and-burlapped plants should be adequate in size, and the wrapping material should be intact and firmly secured (Figure 6-13).
- When the container is carefully pulled away from a container-grown or containerized plant to reveal the root ball, there should be white roots on the outside of the ball. If the plant has become root-bound the roots will begin to circle around the outside of the root ball, and the possibility exists that the roots of the plant, particularly trees, could girdle or kill it (Figure 6-14).
- The plants should be receiving adequate care from the retailer. The soil should be evenly moist so that no drying of the roots or wilting of the leaves has occurred. Conversely, the plants should not be overwatered and allowed to sit in a puddle that could cause root suffocation or disease.
- The plants should have been carefully handled — no broken buds or branches and no scratched or damaged bark. The plants should be stored properly away from drying winds and scalding or freezing temperatures.
- The business should be neat and clean. Walks should be swept, water hoses should be pulled out of the aisles, and hard goods (potting soils, fertilizers, watering equipment) should be stacked, labeled, and priced (Figure 6-15).
- Employees should be able to give knowledgeable answers to questions, or at least be able to get answers for you. They should be willing to help you locate plants or products they don't carry.
- If a guarantee is important to you, find out if one is offered, and decide whether its terms are satisfactory.

As you would in choosing a doctor, dentist, or attorney, take time in selecting plant professionals who will sell you the types of plants and give you the type of service you desire. No industry is without dishonest people, so take the time to shop for plants as a careful and informed customer. In plant

How Important Are Plant Guarantees?

There is some dispute among retail nurseries and garden centers as to whether or not guarantees should be offered for the plants they sell. Many retailers feel that once a plant leaves the premises it is no longer their responsibility, and that not offering a guarantee requires people to be more careful in handling and putting in their plants.

Other retailers unconditionally offer a set-time guarantee on all plants they sell. To assure happy customers who will return again and again and who will speak favorably about their services and products to others, they do not place any major responsibility on the customer. They hope that in offering a guarantee they will help to alleviate the buyer's most common fear — that anything he or she plants will die.

When a guarantee is offered it usually includes one or more of the following restrictions that will classify it as either a limited or an unconditional guarantee:

- The type of plant(s) covered.
- The length of time the plants are covered (one year, three months).
- The season or time of year the plants are covered (e.g., only from March to October).
- Who must plant the plants (the customer, the retailer, a landscape contractor).
- What type of replacement is available (full cash refund, a replacement plant, 50 percent off a replacement plant).

With regard to the type of plants covered, some nurseries cover everything from large trees to small bedding plants. Others only cover "regular" nursery stock — trees and shrubs, plants over a certain dollar value, plants that have been either container-grown or field-dug with soil balls — but not bare-rooted plants. They typically may exclude living Christmas trees (those with attached roots), bedding plants, vegetable transplants, indoor or foliage plants, or plants damaged by summer drought or severe winter weather.

If a guarantee is offered, be sure to save your sales slips and write the date, size, and type of plant purchased on each. Be fair to the retailer and do not take advantage of a guarantee by asking for a replacement of a plant you mishandled. If no guarantee is posted or mentioned, or if you have any doubts, ask what the policy is.

There are pros and cons to guarantees, and the issue will probably never be resolved. Retailers will continue to offer what they feel is fair to most customers, and what realistically they can afford to do financially. It is more important for the customer that a retailer offer good quality, well-maintained plants than a guarantee.

Many retailers with no specific guarantee policy will make some form of reasonable reimbursement or replacement if customers demonstrate that they handled the plants properly or if the retailer can see that the plants were inferior or in less than optimal condition when purchased. How many mass merchandisers, discounters, or grocery stores will do this? How many of them conscientiously maintain the plants until you buy them, or will spend the time with you telling you how to plant and care for the plants? Remember that the purchase price of a plant from a nursery or garden center includes the services of, or advice available from, their trained personnel.

purchases as with any other purchases, you generally get what you pay for.

Be sure that you don't abuse the plants when you transport them and hold them at home prior to planting them. Shield them from wind and sun as much as possible while driving home, especially if they are evergreens or deciduous plants that have leafed out. Store them in a cool, shaded, sheltered place until they can be planted.

Keep the roots of bare-rooted plants moist, cool, and covered, and if planting will be delayed, temporarily pot them up in a moist medium or heel

Figure 6-15. Look for a garden center that is well organized, neat, and clean.

Figure 6-16. Shrubs (roses) temporarily "heeled in" in a mulch pile until they can be planted in a permanent location.

Right

Wrong

Result

Figure 6-17. There is a proper way to dig a planting hole. When the planting hole is dug deeper than the root ball (center), settling will generally occur (bottom). This will leave the plant in a pit — subject to root suffocation during wet periods or stem damage if soil or silt fills in around the stem. The proper way is to set a plant into a hole that is the same depth as the root ball; settling is then avoided and good root development will occur in the upper 10 to 12 inches of soil. In heavy soils (that do not always drain well), you may leave a small portion of the root ball protruding from the soil; protect that small protrusion with a layer of mulch (top).

them (plant them temporarily) in the ground in an area sheltered from the wind (Figure 6-16). Keep the soil balls of balled-and-burlapped, container-grown, processed-balled, and containerized plants evenly moist. Be sure not to drop balled-and-burlapped plants or carry them only by holding the trunks — you could break the root ball.

PROPER PLANTING TECHNIQUES

During the past ten years few aspects of horticulture have received more attention than that of how to properly plant trees and shrubs. Many of our planting practices were "handed down" with little evidence as to how or why they evolved as they did. Recent horticultural research indicates that many of these practices need serious reconsideration, whether we are adding new plants to our landscapes or moving plants within a landscape.

The Planting Hole

The first major change relates to the size and shape of the planting hole. Recommendations now call for a wider and shallower hole that will follow the more lateral and shallow root spread that we now understand most trees and shrubs have.

In general, the hole should be dug to a diameter at least twice that of the root ball or root spread. For example, if the root ball has a 12-inch spread, dig a 24-inch diameter hole. The hole need be no deeper than the depth of the root system or root ball because digging the hole too deep can result in the root ball dropping below the planting level as the soil beneath the ball settles and compacts. Settling too deep can lead to root suffocation or decay if water collects over and around the roots, or if soil washes in over the roots.

In heavy soils that drain poorly, it is often recommended that less than the total root ball be placed in the hole. Under these circumstances a shallow hole can be dug, and the top of the ball that is exposed above ground covered with 2 or 3 inches of mulch for protection (Figure 6-17).

If the hole for a large tree or shrub is being dug with a tree spade, auger, or other piece of power equipment, and a planting hole with a glazed side results (common where the clay content is high), be sure to rough up the side prior to backfilling. A glazed planting hole can act like an in-ground container and keep the roots from penetrating into the surrounding soil. It can also fill up with water, resulting in plant root suffocation or disease as mentioned above.

If the tree or shrub is bare-rooted, prune off any broken, damaged, or diseased roots, then hold the plant in place while you begin to backfill. Hold the plant so that the soil level will be at the same level as it was in the field. There will generally be a color difference on the stem that will indicate this level.

If the plant is balled-and-burlapped, place the ball in the hole and either cut it several times or remove the wrapping material if it is not cotton burlap. Even if biodegradable wrapping material is used, roots will grow out more quickly if the wrapping material is cut or partially removed (at least be sure that it does not sit exposed on the surface where it can quickly dry out). Remove any nails or pins used to hold the ball together, and especially any rope or twine tied around the ball and/or trunk.

If the ball of a large tree or shrub was placed in a wire basket after the ball was wrapped, remove the wire basket prior to placing the root ball in the hole, or clip the basket apart if it is to remain in the hole. Research has shown that wire baskets do not decompose as rapidly as organic materials and can cause serious root deformation (Figure 6-18).

If a field-grown tree or shrub has been dug with a soil ball and placed in a fiber pot, the pot can be planted as long as any margin of the pot that protrudes above ground is removed. Any portion of the pot left above ground can serve to wick water out of the ground, thereby drying the root ball out faster. Fiber pots can be removed if the roots haven't begun to grow into them too extensively, but if much resistance is met in trying to remove the pot, leave it on to avoid root damage. If a field-grown tree or shrub was processed balled,

Figure 6-18. Before the planting hole for this tree is backfilled, both the treated burlap wrap and the wire basket should be cut through.

Figure 6-19. These trees have been machine balled or process balled. The plastic sleeve will not break down easily after planting and must be removed before the root ball is covered with soil in the planting hole.

Figure 6-20. Before you plant a tree that has grown in a container, check to see if major roots have grown up close to the trunk. If so, cut them to avoid girdling in the future. Girdling roots, such as those shown above, may eventually kill this tree.

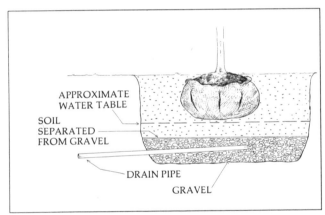

Figure 6-21. Only add gravel to improve the drainage of a planting hole dug in heavy, clay soils. The roots should be entirely above the approximate water table and the backfill soil separated from the gravel in some way (wire mesh, soil separator fabric). There should be no more than 4 to 6 inches of gravel and a drain pipe (a tile pipe works well) that leads down and away from the planting hole. Water will only enter the drain pipe when the soil is very wet, which should improve drainage and eliminate root suffocation.

as mentioned above, remove whatever ball coverings will not decompose. This may be nothing more than the plastic sleeve used to cover the processed ball, or it may mean the wrapping material as well (Figure 6-19).

Be sure to remove the plastic or metal pot or container of container-grown trees and shrubs. Research is inconclusive at this point as to whether the ball or any circling roots should routinely be cut apart or scored. If a circling root is close to the ball surface and so might grow large enough to girdle the stem, cutting through it is recommended (Figure 6-20). A few large trees are grown in wooden boxes that will usually be slow to decompose. Their sides should generally be removed once the tree is situated in the hole.

Backfilling the Hole

The major reason for digging a wide planting hole is to have plenty of soil that can be "fluffed up" or aerated for backfilling around the root system or ball. Where once a variety of organic additions, most notably peat moss, were recommended for incorporation into the backfill soil at some percentage, this is no longer the recommended practice, regardless of the soil or plant type (not even for acid-loving plants such as azaleas).

What is important is to have plenty of well-aerated soil that plant roots can readily penetrate. Amendments often do help to aerate the soil, but they often hold too much water in around the roots, which is often referred to as the "bucket or bathtub effect." In a reverse effect, once many of these organic amendments dry out, they can be very difficult to rewet and even if the soil surrounding the planting hole is moist, the roots may dry out in the dry amended area.

Many plant species whose roots do not do well in overly moist conditions begin to die once their roots penetrate into soggy amended soil (a condition referred to as "wet feet"). In addition, the boundary formed between the amended soil in the planting hole and the surrounding hole often keeps the roots from penetrating beyond the planting hole, reducing the volume of soil from which they can absorb water and nutrients. And, unfortunately, when organic matter is added to backfill soil the backfill material will begin to settle as the organic matter decomposes, causing plants to sink too deep in their planting holes.

Tools To Use For a Landscape Renovation

Many of the tools that will prove necessary and/or helpful if you plan to do some or all of the landscape renovation work yourself may already be in your toolshed: shovels, pruning shears, watering equip-ment. Depending on the size of plants to be moved, or limbs to be pruned, you may find you'll need to rent or purchase some additional tools or equipment. The following is a list of tools you may want to have:

Digging Tools

A *shovel* — preferably with a round point and a long handle, for general digging.

A *garden spade* — with a flat, straight blade, for out-lining and edging.

A *garden fork or spading fork* (the tines are different) — for loosening and aerating soil; very useful for dig-ging perennials.

A *hand trowel* — for digging small plants such as an-nuals and ground covers.

An easy way to keep digging tools clean and free from rust is to run them up and down in a container of sand and old motor oil after each use.

Pruning and Shearing Tools

A *pair of hand pruners* — preferably with bypass or scissor-cut, not anvil-cut blades. Anvil-cut blades do not pass each other, but only meet head-on; fre-quently they do not cut all the way through and re-sult in plant material being torn.

A *pair of lopping shears* — pruning shears with long handles for cutting through thicker stems where more leverage is needed; again preferably with bypass or scissor-cut blades.

A *pruning saw* — for cutting through material too thick for hand shears or loppers.

A *pole pruner* — for reaching branches high up in a tree.

Hedge shears — for doing any type of flat, formal pruning. Use a pair with bumpers between the han-dles to absorb most of the "shock."

A *bottle of alcohol or 10 percent bleach* — for disin-fecting your tools between pruning cuts on diseased material.

Keep the blades of your pruning tools clean and sharp, and file out any nicks. Do not use string trimmers or shears designed as lawn edgers for pruning.

Tools to Move Plants, Soil, Mulch, and Other Garden Supplies

A *wheelbarrow,* wagon, or garden cart.
A *dolly* for moving heavier material.

Watering Tools

Lengths of *hose.*

Sprinklers that can be set to water only planted areas and not walks, patios, etc., and that keep water application low so that loss to wind and evaporation is minimized.

Miscellaneous Tools

Tape measure and labels or survey flags — for measuring and marking beds and plant locations.

Rakes, both garden and leaf — for gathering up debris and smoothing out planting areas.

A *Rototiller* — for working up the soil of large planting areas.

Aerator — for renovating turf areas.

Spreader — for applying fertilizer and certain pesti-cides.

Sprayer — for applying various chemicals.

Lawn mower — for mowing turf and certain types of ground covers.

Hoe — for cutting weeds (keep the blade sharp by filing it occasionally).

Grass clippers or a string trimmer — for trimming edges (when using a string trimmer take care not to hit the stem of any plants). ∎

This same phenomenon can occur due to the interface created between the artificial media in which container-grown plants grow and the sur-rounding soil. The only ways to amend the backfill soil are to substitute good quality topsoil for poor quality subsoil, or to amend an entire planting bed or area with moderate amounts of organic matter or sand so that there is consistency in texture between the soil in the planting hole and the sur-rounding soil.

In general, reserve organic amendments for use as surface mulches, and do not put gravel in the bottom to improve drainage because the reverse will happen. One exception to this involves con-structing a drain below the root ball with a layer of soil between the gravel drain and the root system so that the roots will not grow into the gravel (Figure 6-21).

Backfill the planting hole approximately one-half to two-thirds full, tamp the soil down firmly,

Figure 6-22. To properly wrap a tree start at soil level and proceed in upward overlapping circles to just beneath the lowest branch. In this way, water and precipitation will be shed down the wrapping to the ground.

Fig 6-23. This small tree is in a protected area and should not have been staked. Chances are it will not develop as well in its first year as it would have without staking.

then water the soil well and wait until all of the water has drained through before backfilling the remainder of the hole. This will insure that the backfill soil will be moist and won't dry the roots by absorbing water from them, and will also help to settle out any major air pockets. If the soil is particularly wet when you want to plant, try to wait until it has dried somewhat before digging your hole. Working wet soil can ruin its structure and compact it, causing it to drain poorly, cake over, and shed water.

Another practice generally discouraged in the past at planting time was the use of any type of fertilizer. Organic fertilizers and slow-release inorganic fertilizers (often in compressed or pelletized form) can be incorporated at backfill time. Be sure to follow the recommended rate, and be sure not to use a fast-release inorganic fertilizer that could absorb water from the roots, causing them to "burn." It is hoped that roots will begin to regenerate after planting and therefore an available food source for them is desirable.

Wrapping, Staking, Mulching

Consider wrapping the trunks of thin-barked trees that have been planted in late spring or summer because the bark may heat to temperatures above those to which it has previously been exposed or it could be damaged by excess water loss. Always start wrapping from the soil line upward to just beneath the lowest branch so that water will be shed down the wrapping and not funneled in beneath it where it can cause the bark to decay. Wrap in overlapping spirals that will put two thicknesses of wrapping around the trunk. Whenever possible use a biodegradable material such as burlap or a special tree-wrap paper, and always remove the tree wrap within a year or two of planting (Figure 6-22).

In the past, the recommendation about staking trees was to stake all trees regardless of size. Research has shown that trees should be staked only if they are in an exposed area where they may physically blow over in their planting hole, or if their crown is disproportionately large for their root ball. Trees that do not need to be staked shouldn't be; unstaked trees develop stronger and more flexible stems because they are allowed to move with the wind (Figure 6-23). They also tend to develop stems of larger caliper (diameter) than their staked counterparts.

When staking or guying trees, you can choose from a variety of staking methods and products. Select one that will minimize any damage to the roots or trunk, and where possible, leave the tree an inch or two of space in which to flex. If stakes will be positioned in the planting hole, install them prior to backfilling the soil so that you can see where to put the stakes and avoid driving them into and damaging any roots.

Cover any twine, rope, or wire that is wrapped around the trunk with a protective material, and remove all guying and staking materials after one year (Figure 6-24). If a tree's roots have not been adequately reestablished in a year to the point that they can support the tree, there is something wrong with either the tree, the planting site, or the planting techniques.

All trees and shrubs should be mulched after planting. Mulching serves not only to help conserve soil moisture and keep grass and weed growth/or competition down, but it also keeps the soil temperature cooler in the summer and warmer in the winter, thus extending the time during which root growth will be active. Another important function of mulches is to keep lawn mowers, string trimmers, and other equipment from running into or damaging the trunk or bark (Figure 6-25).

Use 2 to 3 inches of an organic mulch (peat moss, shredded or chunk pine bark, rotted sawdust, compost, pine needles). A mulch deeper than 2 to 3 inches can encourage overly shallow root development, can become waterlogged, and can encourage bark decay and foraging by rodents, especially if piled directly against the tree trunk.

The use of black plastic should be discouraged. Too often the black plastic is wrapped tightly around trees or shrubs, preventing water from getting to their roots (Figure 6-26). Black plastic blocks both water penetration and air. The roots of many plants will begin to suffocate under black plastic. The roots may also grow right at the soil surface where they are more susceptible to freezing or drying, especially if the plastic is later removed.

Newspaper has often been used as a barrier under organic mulches because it allows water to rain through, and because it decomposes. There are now synthetic weed barriers that, although they do not decompose, which in most cases is desirable, they do permit water and air to penetrate. They

Figure 6-24. Guy wires should be covered to avoid cutting or wounding the tree. In this case, old hoses serve as an appropriate wire covering.

Figure 6-25. Trees should be mulched after planting, like the one above, to avoid damage from maintenance equipment.

Figure 6-26. Black plastic mulch is not recommended. When it is pulled tightly around a tree stem, both water and air will not reach the roots. As a result, the roots will try to push their way to the surface where they will be more susceptible to environmental extremes and damage.

Figure 6-27. Rock mulches will probably affect the soil's pH, which could in turn influence the growth of plants in that area. A white gravel mulch will cause dangerous amounts of heat to be radiated up onto a plant's bark and lower leaves.

can be used very successfully under an inch or two of organic material and should be substituted for black plastic.

Most gravel and rock material should be avoided as mulches directly around plants because their general alkaline nature can adversely raise the soil's pH, and because if the materials are light-colored they can reflect light up onto a tree's bark, often causing it to heat to a dangerous temperature (Figure 6-27). Dark rock materials which, unlike dark-colored organic materials, do not hold moisture, will also raise soil temperatures to an undesirable level because they will absorb and hold heat.

Mulches should be used for at least the first few years around newly transplanted trees and shrubs while their roots are reestablishing. Their continued use around plants after that will, as mentioned above, help to minimize equipment damage to the plants.

Remove any tags or labels that have been attached to the plants, whether plastic wraparounds or plastic or paper tabs attached with wire or string. This will keep the labels from girdling the stems (Figure 6-28). If you want to label your plants, place a stake or some other form of more permanent marking in the ground near the base of each plant.

PRUNING

One last major area of change with regard to planting practices: it is neither necessary nor desirable to arbitrarily prune off one-quarter to one-third of the top growth. This practice was recommended in the past to counteract the loss of roots on field-grown trees and shrubs, or to reestablish the "shoot-to-root" ratio (the amount of top growth — stems, leaves — versus the amount of root growth).

Research has shown that unnecessary pruning removes stored sugars and bud-produced growth regulators that are needed to stimulate and support root regeneration. The only pruning that is recommended is pruning that removes broken, damaged, or diseased branches, or that corrects structural defects such as narrow crotch angles and rubbing or crossing branches (Figure 6-29).

In a few species that develop overly twiggy canopies, it is also helpful to thin out a small number of extra branches. Cut smaller branches back to larg-

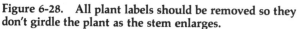
Figure 6-28. All plant labels should be removed so they don't girdle the plant as the stem enlarges.

Figure 6-29. Corrective pruning will open up this recently transplanted tree by eliminating several narrow crotch angles (structural defects).

er branches or to buds growing in the direction of desired new growth, but never remove all of the tips of the branches. If there are sprouts or suckers at the base or on the lower trunk of trees, these should be pruned away (Figure 6-30). If multiple leaders exist on a tree where only one main leader is desired, prune any lesser leaders away leaving only the largest and/or straightest leader. Follow the correct pruning procedures outlined on pages 93–97.

Also, there is no need to treat pruning wounds with any type of commercial wound dressing, latex house paint, shellac, or any of the materials that have been painted or sprayed on pruning cuts in the past. None of the materials currently available help with wound closure, and some can detrimentally seal in excess moisture and insect and disease pests that can be harmful to the plants.

In summary, here is a list of the planting practices that should be followed to increase transplant success.

- Soak bare-rooted plants for an hour or two to rehydrate their roots prior to planting, and do corrective root pruning if necessary. Water the soil of balled-and-burlapped, container-grown, processed-balled, and containerized plants if it is dry.
- Dig a planting hole that is at least twice the diameter of the root ball or spread of the root system, and with the possible exception of a shallower planting hole in heavy clay soils, as deep as the root ball or root spread. Scar the sides of glazed planting holes.
- Remove any containers, ball wrappings, or twine as necessary.

Figure 6-30. The suckers at the base of this small tree should be removed.

Figure 6-31

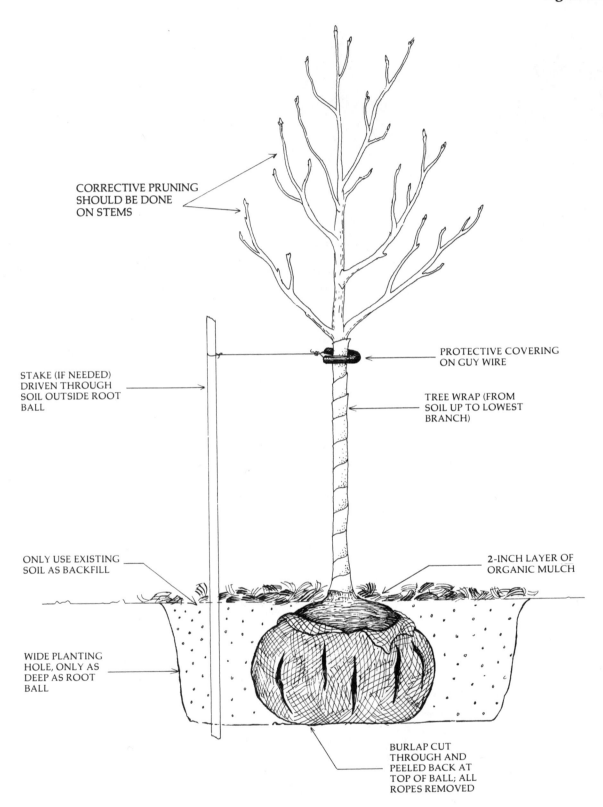

CORRECTIVE PRUNING
SHOULD BE DONE
ON STEMS

PROTECTIVE COVERING
ON GUY WIRE

STAKE (IF NEEDED)
DRIVEN THROUGH
SOIL OUTSIDE ROOT
BALL

TREE WRAP (FROM
SOIL UP TO LOWEST
BRANCH)

ONLY USE EXISTING
SOIL AS BACKFILL

2-INCH LAYER OF
ORGANIC MULCH

WIDE PLANTING
HOLE, ONLY AS
DEEP AS ROOT
BALL

BURLAP CUT
THROUGH AND
PEELED BACK AT
TOP OF BALL; ALL
ROPES REMOVED

Correct Planting Technique

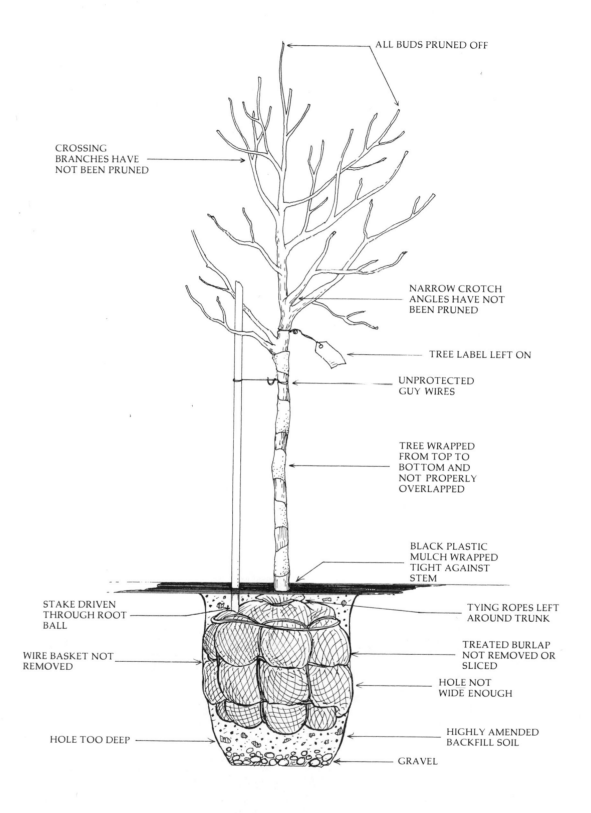

ALL BUDS PRUNED OFF

CROSSING
BRANCHES HAVE
NOT BEEN PRUNED

NARROW CROTCH
ANGLES HAVE NOT
BEEN PRUNED

TREE LABEL LEFT ON

UNPROTECTED
GUY WIRES

TREE WRAPPED
FROM TOP TO
BOTTOM AND
NOT PROPERLY
OVERLAPPED

BLACK PLASTIC
MULCH WRAPPED
TIGHT AGAINST
STEM

STAKE DRIVEN
THROUGH ROOT
BALL

TYING ROPES LEFT
AROUND TRUNK

TREATED BURLAP
NOT REMOVED OR
SLICED

WIRE BASKET NOT
REMOVED

HOLE NOT
WIDE ENOUGH

HOLE TOO DEEP

HIGHLY AMENDED
BACKFILL SOIL

GRAVEL

Incorrect Planting Technique

- In most situations, backfill with well-aerated existing soil, incorporating organic or slow-release fertilizer if desired. Backfill one-half to two-thirds of the planting hole, tamp the soil down, then water the soil and let all water drain through. Then finish backfilling the hole and water again.
- Where desired, form the top of the backfill soil or a layer of mulch into a well to serve as a water reservoir.
- Wrap tree trunks when deemed necessary, but be sure to remove the wrap within a year or two.
- Stake only trees that need staking. Install and attach stakes in such a way as to minimize any root or bark damage. Remove all stakes, guying, and attaching rope or wire within one year.
- Apply 2 to 3 inches of organic mulch with or without an underlying layer of synthetic weed-barrier fabric around all plants. Keep the mulch in place for at least the first few years.
- Prune only to remove undesirable or defective growth. Do not treat pruning wounds with any type of wound dressing.

Figure 6-31 shows correct and incorrect planting techniques.

SEASONAL CONDITIONS

In addition to using proper planting techniques, try to install plants under favorable planting conditions that encourage rapid root regeneration and establishment. This generally means the spring and fall when soil temperatures are warm and soil-moisture content is high, and when most plants show the greatest amount of natural cyclic root growth.

Plants can be successfully planted in the summer, but extra care must be taken to keep the plants from drying out. This will mean frequent watering and possibly shade for the first few months. Likewise plants can be successfully transplanted in the winter, but again they must be protected against drying out, especially if they are evergreens. The exception to typical transplanting times is bare-rooted plants that must be put in while they are dormant in late fall, winter, and early spring.

If several trees and shrubs will be installed at one time, it can be helpful to first mark or stake their planting locations. Follow your scale drawing, and if you see problems with their locations or wish to make adjustments for aesthetic or other reasons, do so now. This will be much easier than having to dig up, move, and replant later on.

If you wish to outline a planting bed before digging it, a piece of rope or watering hose can be used to outline the edge. Here too, adjustments can be made before any digging is started, and once a definite bed outline is established it can even be easily marked on the ground with spray paint, a thin line of flour, ground lime, or a soluble organic material.

Remember that no matter how good the quality or how high the price tag on a tree or shrub, what is most important in a successful transplanting is the use of proper planting techniques and follow-up care.

Figure 6-32. The installation of turf grass and/or ground covers is the final step in a landscape renovation.

How Trees and Shrubs Are Produced

A little knowledge about how trees and shrubs are grown and marketed will help you, as a consumer, make a more educated purchase. There are basically two methods used by the nursery industry to produce the plants we buy. Trees and shrubs are either field-grown — meaning they are grown in the ground — or they are container-grown. Both of these major methods have advantages and disadvantages for both the grower and the consumer.

▲ Shown above are small liners (also known as rooted cuttings or seedlings) that are often planted out-of-doors to mature as field stock. Field stock (right) is grown in the ground until it reaches the desired height or caliper for harvesting.

Until the end of World War II, almost all of the nursery stock grown in North America was field-grown. Field-grown trees and shrubs start as small seedlings or liners (rooted cuttings), or as relatively unbranched whips (taller trees, often 6 feet tall or more), that are planted in the field and dug or harvested when they have reached a desired size. Then, depending on several factors, they are either dug and sold bare-rooted, dug and their roots encased in an "artificial" ball (processed-balled), potted up into a container (containerized), or dug with a ball of soil around their roots and sold balled-and-burlapped (B & B).

Bare-Rooted Plants

Bare-rooted (industry professionals prefer the term "bare-root") trees and shrubs offer several advantages. They can be dug or harvested rather easily, and because they have no soil attached to their roots they are lightweight and easy to handle, ship, and sell. Most of the nursery stock sold by mail is bare-rooted plant material. Bare-rooted trees and shrubs can be a true bargain for the consumer, but there are some disadvantages and restrictions to barerooting.

Only fairly small deciduous trees and shrubs (including roses and fruit trees, shrubs, vines, and brambles) can be dug and handled bare-rooted. Large trees and shrubs generally will not transplant successfully if moved bare-rooted, and no needle or broadleaf evergreen (with the exception of small seedlings) should ever be dug that way. Evergreens have leaves attached that transpire (lose) water which cannot be taken up and replaced by a root system damaged in the digging process. ▶

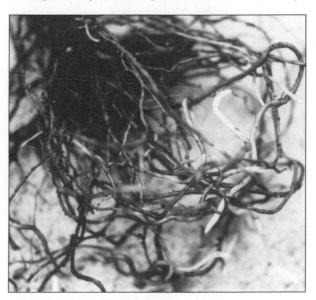

◀ Only small deciduous trees and shrubs can be handled bare-rooted. Note here the desirable white root tips typical of a healthy plant.

Even with small trees and shrubs the time of year during which they can be bare-rooted is limited. Bare-rooting must be done (dug up, shipped, and transplanted) while the plants are dormant, meaning late fall, winter, and early spring. Once deciduous plants begin to break bud in the spring, they must immediately be planted in the ground or potted up into a container if they are bare-rooted.

▶ At right is a load of bare-rooted trees whose root balls have been processed or machine balled, which makes them appear to have been dug with a root ball of soil from the field.

◀ Field-grown, balled-and-burlapped plants are heavier to handle and ship. These trees have been loaded onto pallets to be handled by a fork lift because of their weight.

Containerized Plants

Bare-rooted plants that are potted up into containers are called containerized plants. Containerized trees and shrubs vary from container-grown plants which start as small seedlings (called liners) that are potted up and grown to market size in a container; they may grow in the container for several months to several years; and may even, as they grow, be sized up from a smaller container to a larger one.

Containerized plants start their life in a container when they are already sizeable trees and shrubs, and only a small portion of their older, woody roots comes along from the field to be put in the container. There is nothing wrong with buying containerized plants if they have been held in their containers long enough to assure that good fibrous root systems, which can keep the trees or shrubs alive once they have been transplanted, have had time to regenerate.

A major problem with containerized plants is that they are often potted one day and sold within the next few days. This is far too short a period of time to be sure that sufficient roots exist to sustain the plant.

▶

◀ Larger bare-rooted plants that are potted up for sale are referred to as potted or containerized plants. Note that this plant (a rose) must be pruned to accommodate the container; this could create problems for the plant later if it has not had enough time to grow properly in the container.

The consumer is in essence paying an excessive price for a pot, some potting medium, and a bare-rooted plant that may die very shortly after being transplanted to the landscape.

Containerization only gives the appearance that plants have been container-grown. In some cases the packaging or instructions with the plants will say that they have been potted. In other cases the consumer may be able to tell that the trees or shrubs were containerized because they are potted into biodegradable fiber pots. Typically all true container-grown plants are grown in either plastic or metal containers.

One way to assure yourself that a plant has an adequate root system, be it containerized or container-grown, is to gently remove the container and examine the root system. If the plant is in a fiber pot and considerable resistance is met in trying to remove the pot, assume that new roots have begun to grow and are holding the pot on. Do not try further to remove the pot, or the new roots will be damaged. If the potting medium falls away and reveals an unacceptable root system, don't buy the plant regardless of how it was grown. If the outside of the soil ball is covered with a good growth of fine roots that will generally be white in color (a few species have healthy roots that are tan, red, or brown), the plant should be healthy and transplant well.

Even the roots of container-grown plants may be unacceptable. If removing the pot reveals a lack of roots, they may have been killed by temperature extremes or a lack of moisture. They may also have been destroyed if excessive watering led to root rot.

▲ These containerized blackberries have wilted because they did not have an adequate root system to absorb enough water for good growth after they were dug bare-rooted.

◀ A large bare-rooted tree (flowering dogwood) about to be containerized; its root system is not sufficient to promote good growth.

Processed-Balled Plants

Sometimes bare-rooted plants have an artificial medium (compost, peat moss, sawdust) packed around their roots, and this medium is then shaped and wrapped like a field-grown root ball. Referred to as machine- or shed-balls, or processed-balls, these trees and shrubs, like the containerized plants, give a false impression as to how they were grown and harvested. They are actually field-grown, bare-root harvested, and packaged to look like balled-and-burlapped plants. The very symmetrical shape of their root balls, and the uniformity of root balls from one plant to another may be a clue to their packaging, although balled-and-burlapped plants may have very symmetrical root balls if they are machine dug.

Again, if processed-balled plants are held long enough to assure adequate root regeneration, as with containerized trees and shrubs, they may be very acceptable. Fast-growing plants with shallow, fibrous root systems are those best adapted to containerization and processed-balling. ▶

Even if a containerized or processed-balled plant leafs out this is not a guarantee that new root growth has occurred. The plant may be initially living on stored food and water and may then suddenly die once these reserves are exhausted.

Field-Grown Plants

Large field-grown deciduous trees and shrubs and all evergreens that cannot be dug and handled as bare-rooted or modified bare-rooted plants, must be dug from the ground and their soil/root ball either wrapped or placed temporarily in a container. Consumers should be wary of the wrapping materials. Traditionally, cotton burlap was used because the ball could be left in the burlap at planting and the burlap would then decompose underground so that the roots could grow out into the surrounding soil.

Due in part to the cost of cotton burlap, at present many different materials are used to wrap tree balls. There are treated burlap and plastic burlap-like materials being used, as well as other synthetic materials like nylon carpet backing. Although these materials may be useful because they won't break down while the plant is being held for retail sale, many people do not realize that these materials won't break down when they are planted. Trees may blow over or die years after they are planted because their roots are still restricted within the "artificial" wrapping.

Because of the greater difficulty in harvesting balled-and-burlapped (B & B) field material, and the added shipping weight due to the soil root ball, these plants will be more expensive than bare-rooted plants. Though at one time they too were mainly harvested when they were dormant, many are now harvested year-round with the use of large digging equipment. ▶

▲ This tree has a balled-and-burlapped root ball that is being held temporarily in a plastic pot. The nursery is not making any attempt to disguise this plant as one that has been container grown.

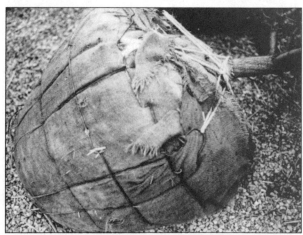

▲ True cotton burlap can be left around the root ball after planting because it will decompose (you might ask, though, whether it has been treated with any chemical preservatives). The metal basket and tying rope should be removed, however.

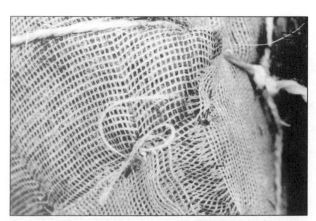

▲ Shown here is synthetic carpet backing material used to wrap a root ball. Because it will not easily decompose, it should be removed or cut before soil is backfilled over the root ball in the planting hole.

Container-Grown Plants

Due to time restrictions, harvesting difficulties, and the added weight of the root ball of balled-and-burlapped plant materials, many trees and shrubs are now grown in containers. An additional reason for container-growing is the fact that you'll get the entire root system with your tree or shrub (with field digging, as much as 98 percent of the plant's root system may be left behind in the ground).

Unfortunately there are also disadvantages to container-grown trees and shrubs. Due to their more intensive cultural requirements (daily watering during the growing season, a need to protect their roots from freezing winter temperatures, etc.), container plants may be a bit more expensive, and container-grown trees rarely develop as large a caliper (diameter) trunk as their field-grown counterparts. When the roots of a container-grown tree reach the outside of the root ball they may begin to circle around the root ball, following the smooth side of the container; if major circling roots develop close to the surface they have the potential to girdle and kill the tree as it grows.

In addition, the artificial or soilless media (shredded pine bark, peat moss, processed sewage sludge, sand, cinders, perlite) in which most container-grown plants are potted can impede penetration of the roots out of the artificial media and into the surrounding soil. Container media generally contain no field soil, or at best only a small percentage because field soil does not drain well when placed aboveground in containers.

	Pros	**Cons**
Bare-Rooted Plants	— Can be dug/harvested easily — They are lightweight, and easy to handle, ship, and sell — Can be a bargain	— Only small deciduous trees and shrubs can be handled bare-rooted — No needle or broadleaf evergreens (except seedlings) can be handled bare-rooted — Must be done while plants are dormant: late fall, winter, or early spring — They are field dug, so lots of roots will be lost
Container-Grown Plants	— The entire root system is maintained — Plants become established and develop good growth in the container	— Have intensive cultural needs: daily watering, protection from cold and winds — Trunk caliper is usually smaller than field-grown plants — Death by circling/girdling roots in the container is possible — Artificial planting media can impede root penetration once planted — Can be a bit more expensive
Containerized Plants	— Best for fast-growing and shallow-rooted plants	— Because plants are already sizable when dug from the field and put into containers, only a portion of the woody roots are saved — Often potted and sold in the span of a few days, which means there is insufficient root growth to sustain the plant
Processed-Balled Plants	— Best for fast-growing and shallow-rooted plants	— Field grown, bare-root harvested, and packaged, to look like balled-and-burlapped plants, but are often not as well established
Field-Grown Plants	— The entire root system is maintained	— More expensive because of difficulties in harvesting B & B Field material — Be conscious of materials used to wrap root balls

ATTENDING TO THE REST OF THE LANDSCAPE

The final step in a landscape renovation involves attending to whatever plant material will cover those exposed areas of ground that have not been planted with trees or shrubs or covered by some form of permanent paving. The plant material to use may be a turf grass, a ground cover, or a combination of plant coverings (Figure 6-32).

Renovating the lawn or ground cover area is left until last because considerable damage may be sustained by this area as nonplant improvements are added, and as plants are removed, moved, or added. Lawn renovation may be desirable for other reasons as well, including a desire to change the grass or ground cover species.

The lawn or ground cover area may also need renovation due to dense weeds, insect, or disease damage, worn areas resulting from heavy foot or vehicle traffic, or the buildup of thatch common to certain species of grass. Where trees and shrubs have grown and provided denser shade, sun-loving species of grass or ground covers may have begun to thin or die out and may need replacing.

The best time of year to renovate a lawn area will depend on the species of grass, and to a lesser extent, the species of ground cover. Where a major renovation is needed it may be desirable to first kill off all existing lawn or ground cover areas with a nonselective herbicide (be careful not to allow spray drift to get on trees, shrubs, and other plants

you value), or dig up any ground cover plants that can be saved.

The lawn area should then be worked up in some way, whether with a fork and rake in a small area, or a Rototiller or small plow in a large area. Take care to minimize damaging any plant root systems as you do this, and don't leave soil areas exposed for too long to minimize erosion from wind or water.

Incorporate any organic matter or sand that might be needed for aeration and/or drainage, and any fertilizer or pH-altering materials that a soil test might indicate as necessary. Then regrade and smooth the area before planting new grass seed, sprigs, or sod, or new ground cover plants. Again various information sources are available with regard to the best species to use, and the most favorable time to do renovation work. Postpone the work if conditions are not the best for rapid reestablishment.

In summary, the most satisfactory order in which to execute most landscape renovations will be the following:

1. Remove plants that cannot be saved, rejuvenated, or moved.

2. Renovate or rejuvenate plants that will remain in place.

3. Move any existing plants that can be saved and used in other locations.

4. Install nonplant improvements such as paving, fencing, pools, and small structures.

5. Select and install all new plant material being added to the renovation plan.

6. Renovate the lawn and ground cover areas.

7

REDUCING THE NEED TO RENOVATE AGAIN BY MAINTAINING HEALTHY PLANTS

The time, energy, and money expended in renovating a landscape — whether you do only the analysis yourself and contract out the rest to a landscape designer or contractor, or whether you dig every hole and prune every plant yourself — represents a sizable investment. Once you are finished you may not want to do anything more than stand back and admire your work. You should, however, quickly set up a program that will keep your renovated landscape looking as good as it does the day it is completed. A small amount of routine monitoring, expenditure, and work will delay or eliminate another major renovation of your landscape.

The best place to start to minimize future renovation work is by or with the adoption of good cultural practices. Poor or nonexistent cultural practices were one of the major areas cited earlier for plant decline, so it's a good idea to learn and begin to use the best practices known. Your beautiful, new renovated landscape will not flourish if it suffers from benign neglect!

WATERING

Start with follow-up care for plants that have just been moved or newly planted. The main reason that newly planted trees and shrubs die is because no one continues to water them once they've been planted. Watering them at planting time and then never again is simply not sufficient.

Trees and shrubs should be watered regularly for at least the first year or two after planting whenever there is not sufficient rainfall. Check local references to see how much rain your area receives on a weekly basis. In most areas (with modifications for soil type or exposure), at least 1 to 1½ inches of water per week, from a combination of rain and supplemental watering, should be available to your landscape plants during the active growing season.

Be sure to adopt good water management practices, such as applying water long enough to saturate the soil to a depth of at least 6 to 8 inches, preferably 1 foot or more, to encourage deep rooting of plants. Try to use irrigation equipment that keeps the water on or as close to the soil surface as possible to decrease the wasteful evaporation of water applied overhead. Be sure to water only target plants, and not the sidewalk, driveway, or patio.

Watch your plants closely to see if they show signs of stress from water deprivation. If they wilt during the day, yet recover at night when the temperature cools down, they are not severely stressed. And if water is in scarce supply, first water plants that are the least tolerant of water stress (annual flowers, small plants, or newly transplanted plants).

Mulch as a Water Conservator

A good way to help preserve the water that is applied is to keep planting beds well mulched (Figure 7-1). This does not mean exceedingly deep layers of mulch, but rather means keeping a fairly consistent depth of mulch in place at all times. Many mulches are organic, which means they are constantly decomposing and compressing, releasing nutrients into the soil, but also necessitating mulch replacement on at least a yearly basis.

Organic mulches are generally preferred because they have a more natural appearance and greater water-holding capacities (Figure 7-2). If inorganic materials such as various gravels or limestone rocks are used, keep in mind that they can adversely alter soil pH, they can be heavy and cumbersome to move, and they may be expensive. As mentioned earlier they do not hold water themselves, and if they are light-colored they can adversely reflect light back onto the plants they surround.

As suggested in chapter 6, a common practice when applying mulches is to apply an additional material under the mulches to enhance weed suppression. Newspaper is an inexpensive barrier that's readily available, but it decomposes in a year or two, and therefore has limited effectiveness in a long-term landscape application.

As a possible replacement for newspaper and for black plastic, the new synthetic materials that have been developed can be used more effectively as underliner materials. They are spun-bonded or woven fabrics that help block weed growth and yet water and air can pass back and forth through them. Though expensive, they can help increase

Figure 7-1. A well mulched planting bed will conserve soil moisture better than exposed soil.

Figure 7-2. Organic mulches have greater water-holding capacities and a more natural appearance. Among the many types of organic mulch that can be used on a home landscape is pine straw, which is shown above.

the efficiency and prolong the life of organic mulches. If black plastic must be used it can be made semiporous by cutting holes in it in the vicinity of plants, but unfortunately weeds will then frequently grow through the holes.

WEED CONTROL

Though mulching is generally the most effective and safest way to control weeds in a landscape, another way is through the use of herbicides (chemical weed killers). Many of these products are available for home use, but they are often specific for either grassy weeds or broadleaf weeds, but not both. You should know exactly what the target weed population is before applying an herbicide. In addition, some herbicides will only kill annual weeds, others may kill both annual and perennial weed species.

The timing of herbicide applications is important in that some must be applied before weed seeds germinate (preemergent), though some can be used after weeds get established (postemergent). Keep in mind that because these products are designed to kill plants, their misuse can result in the death of nontarget plants (flowers, shrubs, trees, grass, vegetables). Always read and follow the label directions carefully for any herbicide, or any other chemical product you use in your landscape or garden.

Keep in mind that weeds are easiest to control by preventing seed germination, or by application of control measures when weeds are small. If you control weeds by hand pulling or hoeing, do it in a manner that disturbs the soil as little as possible, so that other weed seeds aren't brought to the soil surface where they can germinate, and to avoid damaging the roots of shallow-rooted landscape plants. Always remove any weed debris after pulling or weeding so that the weeds can't reroot and weed seeds won't get distributed.

PRUNING

A landscape activity that may prove to be therapeutic for both you and your plants can be pruning. To some people pruning may mean taking a pair of hedge shears and flat-topping a shrub that has grown up over the living room windows, which is

Figure 7-3.   One reason to prune is to remedy plant defects. In this case, corrective pruning would eliminate branches that cross and rub.

Figure 7-4.   Pruning would need to be part of a maintenance routine in order to keep the hedge shown here to a particular size so that it will not interfere with people using the sidewalk or parking area.

Figure 7-5. If you want a plant to take on a particular form (top) or to maintain a special design (bottom), pruning will be a necessary part of that plant's maintenance.

really just lazy chopping of a defenseless plant.

Pruning is the purposeful removal of a plant part in a way that will neither disfigure the plant nor interfere with its healthy growth. Here is a list of many good reasons to prune landscape trees and shrubs.

- To correct the form of a plant by the removal of rubbing and crossing branches, narrow crotch angles between branches, water sprouts, and suckers (Figure 7-3).
- To correct damage from vandalism, adverse weather, construction, insects, or diseases.
- To maintain the plant to a particular size (Figure 7-4).
- To train a plant into a particular form or style (Figure 7-5).
- To rejuvenate or renew an old plant.
- To control flower and fruit production.
- To open a plant up for better air circulation, which could reduce insect and disease problems.
- To remove branches so that more light can get to an area.
- To prevent or correct hazardous situations (Figure 7-6).
- To correct root growth when plants are being installed.

For many of these reasons, pruning can be done at any time of year (Figure 7-7). If a strong wind rips a branch from a tree, the sooner the damage is correctly pruned, the less likely the plant will suffer secondary insect and disease damage and the sooner the desired wound compartmentalization process (see pages 38–39) can take place. For certain reasons, however, there may be better times of the year to prune correctly.

The Pruning Cut

The most important thing to mention about pruning at this point is how to actually make the pruning cut. This is an area that has been researched extensively in recent years, and old recommendations have been radically changed to reflect this new information.

In the past we were told to remove a branch by making a "flush cut" against the trunk or a major branch. This was to insure that no stub was left that could decay and die back, although there was often damage to the bark as we tried to cut as closely as possible (Figure 7-8). It is still undesirable to leave a stub, but do not leave more at the base of the branch than before. Leave what is often seen as a raised area of bark at the base of a branch. This area often looks like dark concentric circles or even a roughened fringe at the branch base (Figure 7-9).

This special area of callus cells — called the *branch collar* — is actually tissue of the trunk or main branch. The branch collar is important in wound closure because it helps to minimize internal decay by the development of a chemical defense barrier. Pruning cuts should be made just outside this branch collar (Figure 7-10). If you are pruning diseased plants, disinfect your pruning equipment after each cut by dipping or spraying it with alcohol or a 10 percent bleach solution.

On some plants you will see a second line or marking that will help to direct your pruning cuts. Often a darkened line of rough bark runs from the branch bark crotch into the trunk bark. This is called the *branch bark ridge* and serves as a second pruning-cut guideline (Figure 7-11). Make your pruning cuts on the outside of the branch collar at a 30- to 45-degree angle to the branch bark ridge.

Though these instructions may sound difficult, once you study the anatomy of a few trees and shrubs, these special areas or markings will be easy to find. A proper cut takes no longer to make than an improper cut, but the consequences can be very different (Figure 7-12).

When only a portion of a branch is being removed, you generally want to make a cut that angles away from, and just slightly above, a bud headed in the direction in which you want new growth to go (Figure 7-13). In most cases such a cut should be above a bud that will produce a new branch and then grow out away from the center of the plant.

Whether pruning away entire main branches, or only portions of small branches, be sure to use pruning equipment that is sharp and large enough for the job. Hedge and lawn-edging shears are not pruning shears and will not give the control needed to make correctly placed pruning cuts. Nor are hand shears large enough for removing larger (those with calipers of 1 inch or more) branches. When larger material must be removed, use loppers or a pruning saw, but for all jobs use equipment that makes a clean cut which extends all the way through the plant part being removed without tearing the plant tissue in the process.

Tree Paints and Dressings

Another area of change relates to the use of materials called pruning paints and wound dressings. Research has shown that although some of these materials may stimulate callus production, they do not prevent decay. To date none of the materials that have been used (ranging from orange shellac and latex house paint to asphalt-based tree wound dressings) have helped to reduce decay, and many have been shown to be detrimental to plants. In some cases they actually seal in decay pathogens against the cut-wound surface and accelerate the decay process.

Figure 7-6. Trees limbs should be kept clear of utility lines. Regular and proper pruning (such as that shown) will prevent a dangerous situation from developing because of branches encroaching on power lines.

Figure 7-7. Although there are prescribed times to prune various plants, it may need to be done at any time of the year in response to an accident or natural disaster.

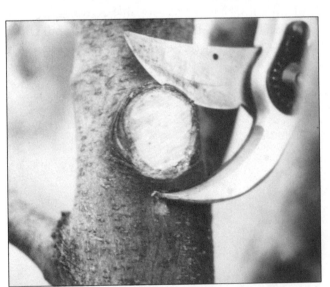

Figure 7-8. Although recommended in the past, "flush cuts" are no longer acceptable because bark is often damaged in the process. A small branch collar is needed for proper wound development.

Make a clean pruning cut and do not bother to apply any material to cover the cut surface. This applies also to correcting large bark wounds on trees where a section of bark has been damaged or ripped away. All that is needed is to neatly cut or scribe around the wound by following its outline. Research has shown that there is no need to scribe a pointed elliptical-shaped area around a wound as was once recommended.

A New Way to Prune

In addition to changes that have occurred with regard to actual pruning techniques, there have been changes in the aesthetics of pruning. With many plants, particularly shrubs that were once sheared back into rigid, formal shapes when they got too big, the current trend is toward maintaining the natural form of the plant whenever possible.

This pruning style is called natural pruning and it means maintaining the normal outline of the plant. When a few branches get too long, instead of cutting the whole plant back into a square or round form, simply trace the "too-long" branches back into the plant crown and remove them where they originate (Figure 7-14). This will lower or reduce the size of the plant and yet leave it with its natural form or outline.

Not only is this more visually pleasing, but it also means less rigorous pruning. In addition, major cut ends won't be visible, and pruning cuts can then be made in the correct ways described above. It is easiest to institute this naturalistic pruning from the start when a plant is young, but even a plant that has been rigidly sheared into an unnatural form can be allowed to grow out of the formal shearing and then repruned naturally.

FEEDING TREES AND SHRUBS

One of the most commonly overlooked cultural practices in the landscape is that of fertilizing trees and shrubs. People almost always feed food-producing plants (vegetables, fruit-bearing trees and shrubs), and frequently feed their lawn grasses, but they often forget that trees and shrubs can benefit from fertilization also.

If a lawn grass fertilizer is being applied on a regular basis it will also be feeding the root systems of any trees or shrubs in the same area. The rates recommended for lawn fertilization are generally high enough to feed both the lawn and the landscape plants, although it is always a good idea to have a soil test run prior to applying fertilizer to be sure what nutrients are needed.

There is no point in applying a more expensive complete fertilizer (one that has three numbers such as 10-10-10, containing nitrogen, phosphorus and potassium respectively) if all that's needed is nitrogen. Nitrogen can be obtained in inexpensive fertilizer forms by itself. A soil test is also important so that a desirable pH (level of soil acidity) can be maintained.

Supplemental fertilizer may need to be applied where a lawn is not fed or where there is no lawn to feed. In addition, trees, shrubs, and perennials in separate beds that do not receive any peripheral lawn fertilizer will also need feeding.

A major misconception regarding plant growth is that tree and shrub roots stop at the drip line (directly under the plant's canopy). This is far from true because plant roots, especially those of trees, can extend great distances beyond their drip lines. In particular, the small fibrous roots that absorb the bulk of a tree's water and nutrients are those that grow a considerable distance beyond it.

There are many fertilizer products available, so check with your local Cooperative Extension Service or garden center about what formulation and rate to use, and at what time or times of the year to apply the fertilizer. Be sure to follow application rates carefully when calibrating equipment with

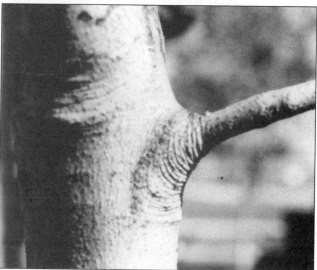

Figure 7-9. The branch collar can be identified by the raised, roughened area at the base of a branch (top), or by a series of concentric circles at the branch base (bottom).

Figure 7-10. Use the branch collar as your guide when pruning (right). After the cut is made, just the collar should remain (below), not a significant stub.

which to apply the fertilizer. Overapplication of fertilizer can result in plant "burn" as the fertilizer actually pulls water out of plant roots. Fertilizer can also burn if it falls on plant leaves and is not washed off.

Fertilization is particularly important for newly installed landscape plants. Young trees and shrubs can often benefit from fertilizer in addition to what they may receive through lawn fertilization. As mentioned in chapter 6, fertilizer that slowly releases its nutrients can even be applied at planting time, a practice that was once discouraged.

Fertilization is also important for landscape plants that have been damaged physically or by a pest organism. Keeping plants strong and healthy will minimize the ability of pest organisms to attack plants, and will help promote the healing process. Whenever you do fertilize, however, be sure that adequate water is available for nutrient uptake. Never fertilize under drought conditions or when water cannot be applied; damaged plants should be fertilized at a reduced rate (generally half the normal rate). A good time to apply fertilizer is when rain is forecast.

A MONITORING ROUTINE

A vital aspect of any home landscape maintenance program should be regular monitoring for things that look amiss. The sooner problems are noticed, correctly identified, and proper control or remedial procedures instituted, the easier prob-

Pest Signs Versus Disease Symptoms

There are two categories of characteristics or clues that can help you to determine what insect or disease pests are bothering your plants. Closely examine the affected plant parts for these clues — the signs and symptoms of pest activity.

A sign is the actual pest present in some form. It could be the actual insect, or a shed or molted skin, or the insect's droppings. For a fungus it could be the threads of the fungus, or the spores or fruiting bodies. That piece or remnant can help in positively identifying the pest, and is much more specific and reliable than pest symptoms.

Insect and disease symptoms are actually plant responses to the activity of a pest. For this reason it is often hard to distinguish between a pathological disease (one caused by a living organism such as an insect or fungus) and a physiological disease (one caused by a nonliving entity such as drought, a premature freeze, chemical drift or compacted soil).

Symptoms can include spots on leaves, dried margins or dead tissue on leaves, twigs with no leaves, wilted plants, or twigs that keep dropping. You do not actually see the insect or disease organism, and can only try to tell from plant manifestations what the actual organism is. The same symptoms can be common for several pest and environmental disorders, and sometimes the problem will be a combination of pest and environmental disorders.

Be sure to look for as many signs and/or symptoms as possible to help distinguish between biotic (caused by a living organism) and abiotic (caused by nonliving, environmental, or cultural factors) diseases, and to help to develop proper control measures. ∎

▲ The most obvious sign of an insect problem is the presence of the insect itself or the home it has built for itself on the host plant.

◀ Leaf spots can be a symptom of a disease organism or a physiological problem.

lems will be to resolve and the less damage and loss will be incurred.

Monitoring can consist of nothing more than a weekly walk around the landscape, but now do a little more investigating than you may have in the past. Turn the leaves on trees and shrubs over and look at the undersides, which is where many insects live and feed. Take note if more twigs than normal seem to be falling off a tree, or if the flower buds on a shrub or perennial flower turn brown and fail to open.

Be sure to get help if you can't determine what is causing irregular or uncharacteristic growth. Nothing makes a control measure more ineffective, futile, and costly than an incorrect identification, especially if a chemical is applied for an insect or disease organism when in fact the problem is a physiological one (drought, air pollution, poor drainage).

If landscape plant problems are indeed diagnosed as being caused by an insect or disease organism, searching immediately for a chemical control is often not only unnecessary, but not even the best control measure. A multifaceted approach to insect and disease control that was developed several years ago is called IPM — Integrated Pest Management. This is a wise approach for both the professional and the homeowner to take with regard to controlling pest problems in their landscapes.

Integrated Pest Management

Integrated Pest Management (IPM) is a concept that has existed for several years. It involves using alternatives to chemical pest controls whenever acceptable and effective alternatives exist. IPM covers all plant pests, including insects, fungi, bacteria, viruses, nematodes, and weeds.

IPM starts with the use of more disease- and insect-tolerant and -resistant plants. Many new plant cultivars have been developed and discovered in recent years that are far superior to the old standards and favorites with regard to pest resistance and tolerance. Whenever these improved cultivars are available they should be used. IPM also involves matching the proper plant with the given environmental conditions. And it includes using the best cultural techniques (proper planting, watering, fertilizing, pruning, and mulching) to keep plants growing vigorously so that they will be better able to withstand pest attacks.

Sanitation is an important component of any successful IPM program. Sanitation includes solar soil sterilization, recycling only "clean" plant debris into the compost pile, roguing (pulling out) diseased or insect-infested plant, and using pest-free seeds and transplants. Sanitation also includes controlling weeds that not only compete with plants for limited resources, but also harbor plant pests.

Although IPM does include the use of chemical controls or pesticides, they should only be used as a last resort after all of the above, and any biological controls, have been tried. Biological controls include insects and fish that eat unwanted weeds, insects that prey on other insects, and diseases that kill insects. Unfortunately, very few economically effective biological controls exist at present.

If all other control measures prove ineffective, then the last control measure to be employed under IPM is the use of chemical pesticides, both organic and inorganic. If chemicals are used they should only be administered as stated on the label. Chemical rates, timing, target plants, and the like are not adjustable — read and follow all label directions exactly.

Controlling Pests

A two-sided approach should be developed for all landscape plant pest problems once they've been correctly identified. First, how do you control or correct the problem right now, and second, how do you control, or preferably prevent the problem in the future? Often a chemical will kill all the targeted insect pests immediately, but it may also kill beneficial insects that are desirable to have because they feed on or parasitize those same pest insects.

Many landscape plants have insect and disease problems that have become commonplace, and if those plants are used repeatedly in surrounding landscapes, control can be difficult unless everyone is working together. Start by educating your neighbors about persistent problems and showing them how you can all work together to reduce pest

Figure 7-11. Another pruning guide is the branch bark ridge, which can be recognized by a ridge of rough, dark tissue that runs from the crotch angle into the trunk area. Make your pruning cuts outside the branch collar at a 30- to 45-degree angle to the branch bark ridge.

problems.

Wherever possible, remove plants that have major pest problems and replace them with varieties or cultivars of the same plant that are more pest resistant or tolerant. Or avoid the problem altogether and just do not use that plant in your landscape again. When you shop for new plants, find out what potential pest problems they have and whether those problems are hard to control. Again in many cases it will be better to simply avoid problem trees and shrubs altogether.

In your landscape, when pest problems do occur, try to remove any damaged plant parts as quickly as possible. Sanitation and cleanup are very important. If you remove the diseased leaves or twigs that can harbor an insect over the winter, then the organism will not reinfect or reinfest your plants the following season. (That means you can't put insect-infested or diseased plant parts on your compost pile. Dispose of the undesired vegetation with the garbage.)

Also along the lines of sanitation, if you have one diseased plant in the midst of several healthy plants, get rid of it before the problem spreads to other plants. This is easy if it means just pulling out one small flowering plant or shrub, but can be difficult if it means removing a large tree. A serious problem in controlling tree diseases is the fact that tree roots will graft together underground and a disease organism can spread from tree to tree by way of the grafted root systems.

A good cultural practice that was mentioned earlier is the conservation of soil moisture through the application of mulches. Mulches also keep weed growth down, and since weeds often harbor insect and disease problems that can also affect

Figure 7-12. Over time, the branch collar of a properly performed pruning cut, like the one shown above, will slowly disappear as the tree's trunk increases in caliper.

Figure 7-13. Directional pruning involves making a diagonal cut slightly above a bud in the area or direction in which you would like new growth to develop.

landscape plants. Therefore, keeping weeds down around your trees and shrubs can help reduce pest problems.

Some pest problems are soil-borne or inhabit the soil. On a small scale it may sometimes be possible to dig out infested or infected soil and replace it with "clean" topsoil. But where this measure is impractical, there are ways, with chemicals and solar heat, to sterilize the soil to kill off the pest organisms, often without damaging desirable organisms.

SMART CHOICE

Be sure to choose and locate plants according to their appropriate growing and environmental needs. If a shrub that needs full sun is put in the shade, or a marginally hardy evergreen tree in the path of winter winds, the plant will be weakened by such adverse growing conditions. It is weakened plants, not healthy plants, that insects and diseases attack. For this reason be sure to employ good cultural techniques to keep your plants growing vigorously, and be sure to closely match the environmental conditions preferred by each plant with the microclimate in which you hope to install the plant.

Despite all of the good preventive measures listed above, your landscape plants will still, from time to time, have pest problems. Whenever possible, try to use a combined "right now" approach that employs biological controls, such as beneficial insects, and that supplements other measures with chemicals when chemical use is warranted.

Always read the labels on chemicals carefully before mixing and applying them. Use them at the right concentration (rate), at the right time, and applied with the right equipment at the right place. Also employ the right safety measures for you, your family, your pets, and any surrounding plants.

There are no insecticides yet available that kill all insect pests, nor fungicides that kill all disease organisms. There generally are appropriate organic and inorganic chemicals available for your use once a correct identification has been made. Again, select whatever control measure will get the job done best, yet minimize negative effects on nontarget organisms and the environment.

Figure 7-14. Natural pruning maintains the normal outline of the plant. This hybrid holly is healthy and has a pleasing shape, but it has some branches that need to be pruned back into the crown.

Recycling Landscape Plants by Propagation

Most people immediately head to a garden center or nursery when they need new or replacement plants for their landscapes. This may not always be necessary if you are interested in saving money, are patient and willing to educate yourself a bit, and if starting or propagating some new plants sounds interesting.

There are basically two ways to start new trees, shrubs, and perennials. You can begin either from seed or from a vegetative piece of the plant (a cutting from a root, stem, or leaf; layering; or grafting or budding). In nature a majority of new plants are propagated by seeds that fall to the ground or are scattered by wind, rain, animals, or birds.

For many of our landscape plants, however, seed propagation may be impractical due to the difficulty in getting certain plant seed to germinate. It may also be undesirable because genetic variation that occurs with seed propagation may produce plants very different in form, growth rate, or color from parent plants. Before trying to propagate any plants whose propagation methods are unfamiliar to you, check a reference so that you won't be disappointed by the results.

For those trees and shrubs that can be seed propagated, fall is the usual seed-collection time. Most seeds of temperate-zone plants need a type of conditioning after harvest before they will germinate. Consult a gardening reference book or encyclopedia for specific conditioning directions. Conditioning is often referred to as stratification, and involves subjecting the seed to moist chilling by either planting it in the ground in a seed bed for the winter, or by mixing it with moist peat moss and refrigerating it for one to four months prior to planting.

Some seeds will not germinate when harvested because their very hard seed coats (seed coverings) block uptake of water or prevent roots from emerging. These seeds will need to be scarified, a process that involves breaking through the hard seed coat with a hot water or acid soak, or abrading the seed coat mechanically.

Most of our landscape shrubs are started from cuttings. A cutting is a piece of root, stem, or leaf that is cut from the desired plant. There are numerous factors to consider when taking cuttings, including what plant parts to use, the best time of year to take the cuttings, the type of rooting medium, and possible root-inducing chemicals (hormones) to use.

With some shrubs the tip of a branch can simply be bent over and buried in the ground where it will then root. This is called layering, and once the layer has rooted it can be cut from the mother plant and function as a new, independent plant.

There are some plants that neither come true from seed nor are easy to root from cuttings or layering, but it may be possible to try grafting or budding. In these procedures, a piece of the desired plant is joined to the branch or root system of another plant. Grafting and budding are generally more complicated for the amateur, and a good propagation reference book may be needed. Most of the popular roses and fruit trees, and many specimen evergreen trees, are produced by this method.

The ground covers and perennials in your landscape also have various propagation methods that must be followed, ranging from the use of seeds to various types of cuttings. With many of these plants, separating or dividing one plant into several smaller plants is often possible — it's a quick and easy way to obtain many new plants.

Before you go out to buy new plants, consider propagating new plants yourself, if you want more of what is already growing in your landscape or perhaps that of a neighbor. You may thoroughly enjoy your propagation efforts. ■

◀ **Propagation is one of the easiest ways to obtain more plants. You can divide them when a plant or clump has grown large (at left are new hosta plants). Or when a plant's flowers are past, it will drop seeds that can be planted to start seedlings the next year (above).**

When Replacement Becomes Necessary

From time to time one or more plants in a landscape may need to be replaced as age or some other factor makes them unattractive or obsolete. These replacements should be made as soon as it is determined that a plant cannot be saved by corrective pruning, treatment for insects, or another method. Too often an otherwise attractive landscape is ruined when a dead tree or shrub is left in place for an extended period of time.

Sometimes it is obvious that older trees are declining and yet they may still have a few functional years left. It can be very difficult to remove an old tree that has had beautiful fall color, or that has given welcomed shade, even though the tree may be losing branches and bark, or may be only partially leafing out. When the need to remove a tree can be anticipated by a few years, sometimes a replacement tree can be planted and encouraged to grow rapidly through diligent care before the existing tree needs to be removed. Obviously the replacement tree cannot be planted in the exact location of the existing tree, but often a location as good or better can be found.

Be sure when positioning a replacement tree that the removal of the old tree will not cause damage to it. You may want to check with an arborist prior to planting a replacement tree to see how and where the old tree can be removed.

Also always consider whether a plant can be moved to a new location rather than removed entirely (see chapter 6 regarding moving plants). Sometimes small new replacement trees and shrubs can be grown temporarily in a "nursery bed" until they can be moved to their permanent locations.

Growth Regulators

Within the professional turf and tree-line clearance businesses the use of some special chemicals are helping to slow plant growth and therefore reduce plant maintenance work. And within the greenhouse industry similar chemicals have been used for years to help keep plants short and well branched.

These chemicals are referred to as plant-growth regulators, and are made both naturally within plants for control of their own growth, and synthetically for application to plants. Various samples of these materials will help prevent florist plants (azaleas, poinsettias) from opening up or getting too tall prior to sale, cut ends on tree branches from sprouting as readily, or grass plants from regrowing as rapidly after mowing.

Although these materials are virtually unknown to homeowners, if they continue to be effective in commercial use, and can be manufactured for a reasonable price, they may in the future be another "tool" available to homeowners for easier management of their landscape plants.

8

DEALING WITH A BRAND-NEW LANDSCAPE

One of the greatest frustrations for the owner of a brand-new house is a landscape that is poorly, improperly, or incompletely planned or planted. A house represents a major investment for any person, and to be greeted by a landscape that doesn't pleasantly or adequately "show it off" can be disheartening, especially if the house and landscape have just been completed. The value of a new house, moreover, seems to have no relationship to the quality of its landscape. Inadequate jobs are done on very expensive homes, as well as more modest ones.

Often the buyer of a new house is unaware that an inadequate job has been done because the landscapes of surrounding houses may look similar. It may not be until a few years after the purchase that the owner begins to realize that had renovation work been undertaken in the very beginning, the landscape would have evolved far better, both aesthetically and in terms of the amount of maintenance required.

JUDGING — AND IMPROVING — THE INITIAL LANDSCAPE

Although many town and municipal building codes require that landscaping be installed for all new house construction, few architects or builders have an adequate knowledge of landscape architecture or design. Even when they do, few put as much money and care into developing a landscape that they put into building the house. Most builders subcontract any landscaping work, and generally set aside a minimal amount for plant purchases and installation. Such a limited landscape budget may in fact be all that is legally required, suggesting that where they exist, code requirements should be changed to upgrade such inadequate new landscapes.

Minimal landscaping budgets generally result in the use of common, inexpensive plants which are put into designs that reflect very little thought. One small shade tree stuck in the middle of the front yard (often right in the sight line of the front door) and five or six evergreens in a row across the front of the house are a poor excuse for a landscape. The landscape looks like an afterthought, something that was done as quickly and cheaply as possible (Figure 8-1).

When a house is sold before it is landscaped, any money that has been set aside for landscaping should be refunded to the homeowner for his or her use in developing the landscape. Where the builder must install a landscape after the sale of the house, the homeowners should be consulted for their opinions and suggestions.

If the money budgeted for landscaping is less

Figure 8-1. Shown here is an example of negligible landscaping that adds nothing to the appearance of the house or the yard.

than needed to complete the landscape, a total design or landscaping plan should be drawn and the most important features installed first. A shade tree placed in an aesthetically enhancing location where it may also favorably modify the environment, plus a few good quality, high-interest shrubs properly placed where they begin to define the total landscape plan constitute a far better start than the situation described above. Homeowners need to be as demanding about the landscape as they are about interior details.

Too often we see an unrealistic placement of plants in the landscapes of new houses. This is typified by the overuse of small and often fast-growing species of plants, and the problem is compounded when most of these plants are installed too close together in an attempt to make a landscape look instantly mature. The result is a landscape that looks overgrown and uncoordinated when it is no more than a few (often less than five) years old.

If a mature look is desired from the start, larger plants in smaller numbers should be purchased. They should be installed and spaced so as to give a finished appearance, but one that will accommodate some additional growth. The danger in this "mature landscape" approach is that maintenance must start from the day the larger plant material is installed in order to keep it from becoming immediately overgrown.

A far better solution is to invest in small, good quality, often slower-growing or dwarf plants, spaced so that ten to fifteen years later the land-

scape will look mature. In doing this, a minimal amount of maintenance each year will help to slow down the rate at which an overgrown landscape could develop. Often temporary plants such as annuals, perennials, or ground covers can be used to fill the large open spaces for the first few years. If annuals are used they should be highly maintained because they can decline fairly quickly and detract from the appearance of the house, especially if used in the front.

The almost exclusive use of evergreen shrubs in the initial front or foundation design too often produces a landscape that lacks textural and color interest, and that leads to the overuse of bright flowering annuals as fillers. As mentioned above, all too often the annual material is inadequately maintained during the growing season and quickly detracts from the appearance of the landscape. When the annuals die out and are removed in the winter, an unsightly void may be left. If the dead plants are left in until new plants are installed the following season, another kind of visual mess may develop.

Evergreen shrubs should be used to form a background for lower-growing deciduous shrubs that bring color and textural variety by way of flowers, fruit, and changing leaf color. If an all-evergreen landscape is designed, the evergreens should be varied in size, shape and leaf color, and texture. Many shades of green are available, as well as leaves with yellow, red, purple, blue, and silver tints, shades, or variegations. In addition, a mixture of needle and broadleaf evergreens can lend nice

Custom Landscape Designs

Many nurseries and garden centers, in an attempt to increase customer service, have developed custom landscape designs that are available as handouts or fact sheets. Each fact sheet features a different basic architectural house style, and comes with a scaled landscape drawing and plant list.

Although this may be an inexpensive way for a contractor or homeowner to obtain a landscape plan, there are inherent problems. One of the most obvious ones is that too many of the same style of house may end up with similar or identical landscapes. This will be particularly true in a new housing development, and can be seen when developers not only use these "canned" plans, but also install the same plants at each house. Try to avoid developing "copycat" landscapes.

With regard to using the same plants, most of these prepared plans offer only one plant suggestion for each planting area that is designated, and frequently overuse evergreens at the expense of color and textural variation. A way to improve these plans is to make alternative selections for each planting area, and to determine what plant material combina-tions are particularly effective together.

Most of the prepared plans are drawn predominantly with straight line beds and straight lines of plants. Landscapes are not only more pleasing and interesting to view, but also easier to maintain, when curved lines are used. In addition, with straight rows of plants it is far more obvious if one plant dies or has a different growth rate than if the plants are spaced in nonlinear groups.

In general the prepared plans do not suggest what size plant to buy (1-gallon versus 3-gallon shrub, 3-foot versus 1-inch caliper tree, etc.), nor do they tell you how many years it will take plants of a particular size to reach maturity or to grow to the size shown on the plan. The plans generally show plants touching or overlapping, and this is not where a new landscape should start because major maintenance will become immediately necessary.

Most nurseries and garden centers offer some form of design service. Many will reimburse, or apply to the cost of buying plants, the amount paid for a landscape design. You will benefit from a landscape design custom-tailored to your house and needs. ∎

---

textural contrast.

Along these same lines, the one tree selected for the front yard is often a fast-growing shade tree that lacks multiseasonal interest, such as attractive spring flowers combined with good fall color or interesting winter bark. Here again, it is better to invest in a small, but better quality (higher-interest) tree. Such a tree can be encouraged to grow at its maximum growth rate with proper watering, fertilizing, mulching, and other cultural practices.

CONSTRUCTION DAMAGE AND TRAUMA TO TREES AND PLANTS

Damage incurred during the construction of a new house can lead to both immediate and long-term problems for the new homeowner. Damage may be observed in the form of cut roots or stripped bark on existing trees that were designated to be saved, or may be far more subtle, such as the removal and nonreplacement of topsoil (Figure 8-2).

Homeowners generally pay much more for a "wooded" lot than for one that is treeless (Figure 8-3). A higher price may be justified as long as the homeowner is realistic about which plants are to be saved, and as long as the contractor makes a concerted effort to minimize damage to the plants designated to be saved.

Trees on a wooded site, especially if they comprise a native stand, are accustomed to growing under a particular set of environmental conditions, such as shade, forest litter as mulch, or buffered wind. When construction begins, those conditions are disturbed or altered, and the "artificial woods" that are created provide less favorable growing conditions and increased stress.

Preserving the root *environment* of the trees to be saved should be a top priority. Where the root zone must be tampered with, precautions should be taken prior to construction to minimize any disturbances. Keep in mind that the competition (for water, nutrients, and sun) which exists between trees in a wooded environment has restricted their root systems in comparison to their successful counterparts growing in less competitive, more open landscape situations. When wooded areas are opened up and trees thinned out, the trees left in place may have root systems less able to adapt to the new, more stressful conditions in which they

Figure 8-2. These trees and their roots have sustained damage because ditches had to be dug for water lines.

Figure 8-3. This is an expensive piece of property because woods surround the house and a number of trees were preserved for the yard area during construction.

are then expected to grow.

Unfortunately, a real assessment of existing plants, with regard to their actual condition, their potential life expectancy, and the value of their species, is rarely done. In most cases a few large trees will be saved, and the small trees will be marked for removal. Often this is the reverse of what should be done because the large trees may be old and declining, and some of the smaller specimens may grow into excellent trees with a bit of judicious clearing and pruning (Figure 8-4). Young

trees will almost always adapt to environmental changes better and more readily than old trees of the same species. In addition, young trees will be easier to remove and replace at a later time should the need arise after construction.

Whether or not the trees to be saved are of a desirable species is frequently overlooked — size seems to be the prime determining factor in what will be saved. Here the help of a trained arborist (many large cities employ one, or a private arborist could be hired), horticulturist, forester, or extension service agent could save the homeowner the aggravation of seeing purchased trees die. It could also save the expense of having dead trees removed and new ones planted. The cost of a consultation prior to construction could result in significant long-term savings.

THE VALUE OF TREES

Trees contribute more to a landscape than just beauty and environmental modification (shade, temperature moderation, air pollution filtration, release of oxygen, precipitation interception and absorption, wind redirection or screening). Trees help to increase the value of a property, to screen out undesirable views or accent a desirable one, to increase the amount of privacy, to stabilize the soil and reduce erosion, to buffer noise and glare, and to feed and shelter wildlife and birds, many of which eat undesirable insects.

Trees, and plants in general, also alter our perception of the environment. When plants are present, our perception of most things improves and we derive a psychological boost or sense of well-being from their presence. Such a quality-of-life feature is extremely important to those who wish to reduce stress by having a place of beauty they can retreat to, and to those who want to preserve a piece of our rapidly shrinking natural landscape.

When considering which trees to save, take into account their species relative to landscape contributions such as flowers, attractive bark, fall color, crown shade, and shade density. In addition, recognize their negative landscape attributes, such as litter created by large leaves, fruit, or twigs, or the insects and diseases that can attack them. Also remember that trees will continue to grow and therefore their roots may seek out water and sewer lines or may cause paving to crack or buckle.

Evaluate the health and vigor of all trees in terms of their current age and life expectancy. Also look at their current condition relative to fire, lightning, and other hazards; insect and disease damage; and miscellaneous wounds (Figure 8-5). How is their structure (crown density, trunk straightness, and branch crotch angles) and wood strength (relative to splitting)? How is their foliage (relative to size, color, and retention) and urban stress tolerance (relative to pollution and vandalism)? Tree species that are native or have grown on a wooded site

Figure 8-4. Some of the trees shown here have ribbons tied around them to indicate that they should be saved. It does not appear that a careful species evaluation was done because mostly older trees have been designated. Oftentimes smaller trees will develop better than more mature specimens that may well be at the end of their normal life span and may not recover as well from construction damage.

naturally are generally better suited for the site than introduced species unless conditions are significantly changed.

A house should not be situated on a lot before trees are evaluated. If the placement of the house, driveway, and other permanent features is flexible, several plans should be drawn to see which will satisfactorily accommodate both the buildings and the trees one desires to save. In most situations a compromise arrangement can be found, but be sure that the cost of saving trees does not exceed the cost of replacing those same trees.

Appreciate the fact that keeping a building lot in a "wooded" state may mean that something else may need to be sacrificed. A good example is the effect that shade from such trees, and the competition from their roots, can have on attempts to establish a stand of grass. Cultivation of a thick, green lawn can be very difficult, if not impossible, under many wooded situations. As the trees continue to grow and the shade they lend increases, underlying vegetation may have even greater difficulty surviving unless it is very shade tolerant.

If the lot cannot be rearranged and yet one or more trees are worth saving, investigate the cost of digging the tree with a tree spade and planting it elsewhere or holding it and replanting it after all construction is completed. A valuable tree in the wrong place will only cause problems.

Preventing Damage to Site Trees

There is more to saving a tree than roping off a "No Trespassing" area a foot from the tree's trunk. Most tree roots are not only shallow (in the top 6 inches to 2 feet of soil), but extend out far beyond the drip line of the crown (Figure 8-6). In most cases root protection is the key to saving existing trees.

Trees to be saved should be physically separated from the grading and building process as much as possible. This can be done by putting a fence several feet away from the trunks to prevent equipment and supplies from touching the trees. In addition, attempts to add or remove soil should be discouraged, as should conditions that compact the soil over tree roots.

Probably the greatest amount of damage to trees occurs when equipment hits them, breaking or tearing away branches and bark; when roots are cut during cut-and-fill or trenching; and when the soil level over their roots is significantly raised or

Figure 8-5. It is unfortunate that this tree was retained at the site of this new home. Not only does it adversely dominate the front of the home because it is unattractive, but it is not a vigorous tree and could create a hazard by dropping limbs or falling over.

lowered, and/or the soil compacted (Figure 8-7). It can be surprising how shallow tree roots actually are (Figure 8-8). Many tree species can tolerate no more than an inch or two of change in the soil level (grade) due either to the exposure of shallow feeder roots if soil is removed, or the suffocation of shallow roots if too much soil is added (roots need oxygen to carry on essential metabolic processes; Figure 8-9).

An easy way to tell if excess fill soil has been added is to look for the natural flare or buttress at the base of a tree (Figure 8-10). If the tree is straight where the soil line hits it, excess soil has been piled over its roots (Figure 8-11). Soil has obviously been removed if major portions of the root system are visible.

Compaction is also detrimental because it reduces the pore spaces in the soil that hold air and moisture. Compaction can change both the ability of the soil to "take up" water needed by the trees' roots and the ability of the soil to drain away excess water. Both reduced uptake and reduced drainage of water will be detrimental not only to existing trees, but also to plants that will be added to the landscape (Figure 8-12). This phenomenon will be evident if it is difficult to establish a lawn, whether from seed or sod, and to get new plants to successfully transplant and grow. All final grading around trees should be done by hand rather than with heavy equipment.

The smaller the lot, the greater is the potential for damage to large trees, and the less the likelihood of adequately preserving them. In addition, the likelihood of damage to the house also increases as large trees begin to die, dropping branches or even breaking or blowing over in storms. The latter should be of utmost concern if major roots were cut during trenching for water lines and utilities. Whenever possible a tunnel should be run a few feet (3 to 4 feet at least) beneath a tree for such lines rather than destroying roots by digging a trench.

Another form of damage may result from a change in drainage patterns. When drainage patterns are changed because of grading, more or less water may be available to the trees than before. Tree damage can result from the paving of surrounding areas because the volume of water running off the paved areas (added to the watershed from the house during rainfall) will create a larger volume of water. It will need to drain through a

Figure 8-6. An inadequate amount of space has been roped off here to really protect these trees from root damage.

Figure 8-7. The tree well shown here indicate that a grade change was made. If roots were covered with too much soil the tree may die because important feeder roots were suffocated.

smaller open area or into a smaller volume of soil than before. This excess moisture can be particularly detrimental if compacted soil causes it to puddle and drain away slowly.

Another form of damage relating to water is the effect of grading on the water table. Water tables generally rise to reestablish their original depth from the surface of the ground when fill is added, and conversely drop back to their original depth if the grade is lowered. When the water table drops, trees may be subjected to drought-type conditions. When the water table rises, the level of the saturated zone of soil above the water table also rises. In this case, a lack of oxygen can cause roots to suffocate or drown.

Damage can be caused by the simple removal of trees, and by thinning surrounding trees and undergrowth. Trees to be saved may be exposed to stronger than usual winds that could cause damage as limbs break or trees blow over (Figure 8-13). In addition, thinning and removing trees and brush will open up an area more, so that the soil beneath the trees dries out faster, especially if the leaf litter that naturally existed under the trees was removed or plowed under (Figure 8-14). And if the litter isn't replaced by some other form of mulch, the drying-out problem will be compounded.

In thinning trees out, care must be taken to insure that the trees being removed do not fall on trees to be saved. Have an experienced arborist do the tree removal, or be sure that whoever removes the trees knows how to notch them, and if necessary, rope or guy them, to avoid damaging trees that will be retained. Protect trees from careless pruning or topping undertaken to make way for overhead utility lines or to give clearance for equipment. Also, avoid leaving one large tree standing alone — a lightning hazard may be created (Figure 8-15). An interesting phenomenon is the grafting of tree roots together underground. One tree may actually obtain part of its water and nutrients from a neighboring tree, and may therefore decline or die if that tree is removed.

Signs of tree stress caused by construction changes to the environment and/or damage to the trees will include premature fall coloration and leaf drop, reduced leaf size, increased twig dieback, increased or sudden susceptibility to insects and diseases, sucker growth on large branches and the trunk, and "stagheading" or the death of large scaffold branches that results in random large branches standing dead in a tree's crown. Depending on the type and extent of environmental changes and tree injury, these signs may show up soon after the damage has occurred or may reveal themselves slowly over an extended period of time.

Figure 8-8. Even the root systems of very large trees can be shallow, as evidenced by this shallow "mat" of roots pulled up when this tree fell over.

Figure 8-9. Tree roots that are exposed as a result of lowering the grade at a construction site may suffer environmental damage, which could consequently traumatize the tree.

Figure 8-10. The natural flare at the base of this tree shows that the grade was not changed.

Figure 8-11. The buttress at the base of this tree is not visible, which proves that the grade was raised.

Figure 8-12. When excess water is not absorbed or drained away, it could be evidence of soil compaction. If the soil is so compacted and hard that not even water can penetrate it, then oxygen does not reach tree and plant roots and they will eventually die.

CONTRACTOR-RELATED DAMAGE

If you drive by new home construction sites and notice the piles of debris that collect on these sites, it's clear that damage can occur in new landscapes because contractors fail to remove or dispose of waste materials properly. Additionally, they can inflict damage when such materials are piled around and against trees (Figure 8-16).

Contractor Improprieties

Often a homeowner will unearth cement, bricks, wiring, packaging materials, buckets, or lengths of wood that the contractor buried when the finished grading was done. Not only does this increase the homeowner's work when these materials must then be disposed of, but materials that are not unearthed may interfere with plant growth due to changes in soil pH and/or nutrient availability. Some of the materials may even be "poisonous" and kill the plants outright, or the plants may die because they were damaged when debris was buried.

Buried materials may also cause problems as the ground settles where these materials have decomposed and/or the area above them has been compacted by precipitation and foot or vehicular traffic. Contractors should be required to dispose of all waste materials off-site, and should also be prohibited from burning waste materials on-site because of toxic residues that may be left behind, or the potential of fire damage to existing plants.

Contractors should also be prohibited from washing out cement mixers and tools on the ground around trees, especially those species that grow best in acid soil (Figure 8-17). The residue of cement materials are alkaline in nature and will cause the soil pH to rise, which can cause the leaves of acid-loving plants to become chlorotic (pale green or yellowish leaf coloration), or result in stunted plant growth. The same phenomenon will occur when marble chips or crushed bluestone is used for gravel driveways (Figure 8-18).

Loss of Topsoil

Removal and nonreplacement of any topsoil that may have existed on a building site is a frequent contributor to plant death (Figure 8-19). Contractors often strip away and sell any "decent" topsoil that exists on a building site, and then simply leave the subsoil as the finished grade soil. Prospective homeowners should require contractors to either initially remove as little topsoil as possible, or to stockpile any topsoil that must be moved in the building process so that it can then be used in the final grading.

What the homeowner gets when the topsoil is removed is a substandard growing medium, one that frequently has a high clay content. This lesser-grade subsoil will often puddle and drain poorly after a rain, and may dry out so thoroughly during drought conditions that it will crack open and become very hard to rewet. Subsoil is almost always a far inferior medium for plant growth, one in which root systems struggle to reestablish themselves before harsh environmental conditions impact upon them. One good indicator of this problem is repeated failure in establishing a turf grass, whether attempts are made by seeding or by sodding.

PLANT SELECTION AND CARE FOR A NEW LANDSCAPE

Poor coordination of plant species with the existing environmental conditions causes many plants added to a new landscape to die. Building contractors or landscapers often fail to note the environmental conditions — soil type, pH, moisture-holding capacity and drainage, amount of sun and shade, and prevailing wind direction — of the finished site. Each site will have its own microclimate and plants should be selected accordingly.

Plants that may thrive in an established neighborhood where the soil has been rehabilitated over time and where tall trees lend a degree of shade, may simply die on a new site one block away where the topsoil was removed and no trees were left standing. There are plants that will survive virtually any environmental conditions, but the condition of most new building sites are rarely conducive to healthy plant growth and the cheap, fast-growing plants that are quickly put in to finish most jobs, will struggle to survive.

Even if plants are selected that can survive the hostile environment of most new homesites, either poor planting techniques or limited (or nonexistent) follow-up maintenance may doom them to death. Since most planting jobs are hurried, little

Figure 8-13. The natural environment of the trees shown here is dramatically different as part of a home site than as part of a wooded area. Because of the change, the trees may respond differently to a new set of environmental conditions.

Figure 8-14. It is important to remember that the leaf litter found under trees in a wooded area (above) is a crucial mulch that helps to preserve necessary moisture. When woods are transformed into home sites, a substitute mulch will be necessary.

Figure 8-15. An improperly pruned (topped) tree stands as a solitary lightning rod — a very hazardous situation.

Figure 8-17. Careless disposal of cement residue can adversely affect soil pH, and could kill acid-loving plants.

Figure 8-16. Construction materials should not be piled under or against trees that are meant to be saved.

Exchanging Plants

If you are dissatisfied with some of the plants used in your landscape, why not try to trade them in for ones that are more desirable? Try to find out who sold, purchased, and/or installed the plants and see if some sort of trade-in or return deal can be worked out.

The feasibility of such an arrangement will depend in great part on the size of the plants, the time of year, the way the plants were produced (container-grown versus field-grown), and, naturally, the willingness of the person who sold or installed them. If a reputable nursery installed the plants, they may at least be willing to take the plants back as a trade-in on something different.

Container-grown plants will generally be the easiest to dig up, especially if the plants have been in the ground no more than a month or two. In that short a period of time few plants will have put out enough new root growth to make it difficult to dig out the original root ball.

If the plants were field-grown, the way in which they were harvested and marketed will determine how feasible digging and exchanging them might be. If the plants were harvested and transplanted bare-rooted, digging would be the most successful method from late fall until early spring while they are dormant. If much new root growth has developed, they shouldn't be bare-rooted again, but should be dug with a ball of soil around the roots.

If small trees or shrubs that were field-grown were dug with a soil ball, the material used to wrap the ball and the subsequent handling during transplanting will impact on redigging success. If the ball was wrapped with cotton burlap that was left fairly intact at planting time, the ball may be easy to uncover and lift.

If, however, the ball was wrapped in a noncotton and/or nonbiodegradable material (a plastic or nylon material such as synthetic burlap or carpet backing), lifting would in great part depend on whether the nonbiodegradable material was cut or entirely removed from around the ball according to proper planting techniques. If it was not cut and/or removed, lifting may be easy. When the balling fabric has been removed, the ball will need to be rewrapped. Such a digging and rewrapping operation is generally better left to an experienced nurseryman. This type of digging should also be done when the plants are dormant, especially if they are evergreens.

Digging and trading back or exchanging landscape plants has some risks, but with the right plants at the right time of year, it can be successful. Not only will the plants be saved, but they will have some monetary value.

If the landscaper or personnel from the nursery won't consider a trade-in or exchange, perhaps a neighbor would be interested in them, or they might interest someone at a garage sale. Just be sure to let a potential buyer know the history of their redigging and suggest to them how to handle the plants for increased transplanting success.

Though the idea of digging up and exchanging or selling plants from a new landscape may sound unorthodox, it can be of benefit to all.

▶ The plants shown here are overgrown, but they are healthy. Chances are good that when a landscape renovation takes place, a local nursery or landscape contractor might accept some of these plants as trade-ins or purchase them outright.

Figure 8-18. Crushed stone intended for driveways and paths should be confined to those areas and not allowed to spill around or near plants where it will eventually change the soil pH.

attempt may be made to dig out buried debris, or to dig an adequately large planting hole. In addition, lack of care in handling the root ball of plants, or failure to use other handling or planting techniques that might improve transplanting success, will result in the death of many plants.

Ironically, one frequent planting practice, the staking of trees and large shrubs, is often unnecessary, and is one way in which time and money could be saved and put toward other planting practices or the purchase of better quality plant material. The same applies to the practice of amending backfill soil as mentioned in chapter 6.

Even if plants are properly installed in a new landscape, they may quickly deteriorate because no provisions are made for follow-up maintenance. The person hired to plant the plants did just that — planted the plants. With luck the plants were at least watered and mulched to help them get started. But what if no rains falls after the landscape is installed? Was anyone hired to come back and follow up on the planting job with some form of routine maintenance, which might amount to no more than a once-a-week deep watering? Probably not, and therefore even if the best quality plants were installed using the best planting techniques, the failure of someone to simply water the plants may kill the new landscape. This will be especially true if the landscape is installed in late spring or during the summer when the environment is likely to be the most stressful.

Figure 8-19. It is apparent that topsoil has been stripped from this building site because tree roots have been exposed. The consequence may be that many of the plants shown here will suffer.

DO A SCALE DRAWING

In light of all these problems, what should the new homeowner do? Complaining to the builder or landscaper will rarely give any satisfaction unless something different was specified in the contract. Frequently what has been installed as a landscape is all that's legally required.

Realize that the best approach is probably to treat the brand-new landscape like any landscape needing renovation. As described earlier in the book, start by doing a scale drawing of the property, house, site details, and any plants that have been saved or added to the landscape. Do not draw the plants to their present size, but to a mature size or a size they could be expected to attain ten to fifteen years from now. That will give a better indication of how quickly they may outgrow their location, or whether they may be used as they presently exist.

If the new plants added to the landscape have been in the ground for no more than six months, the amount of root regeneration or new root growth that has occurred may not be substantial, and the plants may therefore be relatively easy to move to more appropriate locations. Complete the site and family needs analyses, and proceed to de-sign a new landscape as if the existing landscape was well established instead of only a few months or a year old.

IN CONCLUSION

The major reasons that new landscapes are inadequate or begin to decline from the start are listed below.

- Building codes that require landscaping with all new house construction.
- Unrealistic placement of fast-growing plants.
- The almost exclusive use of evergreens in the foundation plantings.
- Damage to existing plants, the soil, and the environment during house construction.
- Failure of contractors to properly remove or dispose of construction debris.
- Removal and nonreplacement of any topsoil that existed on the site.
- Poor coordination of new landscape plants with the existing environmental conditions of the site.
- Poor planting techniques, and/or limited (or nonexistent) follow-up maintenance.

9

VIEWING THE COMPLETED JOB

When you first thought about renovating your landscape you may have envisioned no more than pruning back a few shrubs, removing a dead or dying tree or two, and installing a few new plants. This is the type of renovation job many homeowners undertake, but unfortunately what happens is that they end up doing one type of renovation job or another on a regular basis (Figure 9-1).

It's far better if a homeowner periodically evaluates the entire landscape, realizing that landscapes are not static, but instead dynamic combinations of plants and physical forces that are constantly undergoing change. This applies not only to their own landscapes but also to those that surround them.

If you have followed the suggestions in this book, and have done not only the digging and pruning, but also the analyzing, listing, and designing, you should have a new landscape that is not only more attractive and functional, but one that has also increased the value of your property and given you a sense of accomplishment and satisfaction. With luck you have also gained an appreciation for why good quality landscape plants are not cheap, and why landscaping and maintenance services may initially seem expensive.

Because of the time, labor, and money you have invested in your renovated landscape, the following list is offered to help you protect and maintain your investment.

- Reevaluate your landscape regularly and undertake whatever small renovation projects may be necessary from time to time in order to preserve it and to avoid having to do any unnecessary major renovations again in the future (Figure 9-2).
- Realize that plants have finite functional lives; be willing to replace them as needed.
- Carefully match the environmental needs of plants with the conditions available.
- Be an educated shopper when purchasing landscape plants, equipment, and supplies.
- Use proper planting techniques and give adequate follow-up care to help plants reestablish quickly and successfully.
- Adopt proper cultural practices that will keep your landscape plants healthy and vigorous, as well as decrease the amount of necessary maintenance.
- Monitor frequently for pest and environmental problems, and adopt proper control measures.
- Use chemicals safely and effectively in the landscape, and try to substitute cultural practices

The 10 Steps to a Successful Landscape Renovation

1. Analyze plants for problems

2. Analyze plants for conditions

3. Draw existing landscape

4. Analyze family needs

5. Decide fate of existing plants

6. Coordinate existing landscape with future needs

7. Design renovated landscape

8. Develop renovation installation plan, budget, and calendar

9. Do renovation work

10. Develop maintenance plan for "new landscape"

whenever available and appropriate.

- Consider the impact of your actions not only on your own landscape, but on the landscapes of others in your area.

- Avoid carelessly damaging your landscape plants, and minimize the damage incurred by forces beyond your control as quickly as possible.

- Keep up-to-date about new plants, new practices, and new materials that will make your landscape more attractive and functional.

- Seek professional help and advice whenever you are unsure about a particular plant problem or landscape situation.

- Share your knowledge and experiences with others to enhance not only your personal landscape, but also other landscapes you frequent and enjoy.

- Respect the plants in your landscape and do all you can to help them, recognizing that they are very special, yet wholly silent and undemanding living organisms contributing to the world around you.

Figure 9-1. **Unfortunately, this landscape needs more than pruning. A complete landscape renovation is needed to add interest, variety, and to complement the home and property.**

Figure 9-2. The adoption of good cultural practices will keep any landscape attractive for years to come with minimal maintenance. Such a well-designed and maintained landscape will add value to the property and give pride to the homeowner.

Index

Other Garden Way Publishing Books You Will Enjoy

A Garden of Wildflowers by Henry W. Art. How to propagate 101 native species. Art's lucid text is complemented by botanically accurate drawings. Illustrations, maps, tables; $12.95 (paper), order # 405-0.

The Wildflower Gardener's Guide, Northeastern edition, by Henry W. Art. An authoritative guide to the 32 native species found in the northeastern quarter of North America. Color photographs, drawings, appendixes, index; $9.95 (paper), order # 439-5.

Let's Grow! by Linda Tilgner. Seventy-two garden projects to enjoy with children of all ages and abilities. Wonderful photographs, drawings, index; $10.95 (paper), order # 470-0.

Tips for the Lazy Gardener by Linda Tilgner. An engaging and enjoyable volume for those who want to cut down on the chores and enjoy their gardens more. Drawings, index; $4.95, order # 390-0.

Successful Perennial Gardening by Lewis & Nancy Hill. A thorough and entertaining book on everyone's favorite type of gardening. In three parts: how to grow, maintain, and propagate; 16 theme gardens; 175 species descriptions. Color photographs, botanical and garden drawings, lists, chart, index; $16.95 (paper), order # 472-7.

Pruning Simplified, Updated Edition, by Lewis Hill. A professional nurseryman gives you the knowledge and confidence to do a good and proper pruning job. How to prune trees, shrubs, flowers, vines, house and garden plants, and more. Drawings, index; $12.95 (paper), order # 417-4.

Cold-Climate Gardening by Lewis Hill. How to extend your growing season — no matter how harsh your climate or microclimate — and get the most out of your vegetable and landscape plants. Photographs, drawings, index; $9.95 (paper), order # 441-7.

Sleeping With a Sunflower by Louise Riotte. Gardening lore, knowledge, and decades of experience from a popular garden writer. Drawings, charts, recipes, index; $6.95 (paper), order # 502-2.

Blue Corn & Square Tomatoes by Rebecca Rupp. Little-known facts about 20 common garden vegetables makes for enjoyable and fascinating reading. Drawings, index; $9.95 (paper), order # 505-7.

Peter Chan's Magical Landscape by Peter Chan. Landscape advice from a master at the craft of transforming a landscape into a place of beauty — especially for those with limited space. Color photographs, drawings, charts, index; $10.95 (paper), order # 455-7.

The Beautiful Food Garden by Kate Rogers Gessert. How to landscape with vegetables, herbs, fruits, and flowers. Judged the best general gardening book in 1983 by the Garden Writers of America. Color photographs, drawings, photos, charts, index; $12.95 (paper), order # 461-1.

These books are available at your bookstore, farm store, garden center, or directly from Garden Way Publishing, Schoolhouse Road, Pownal, Vermont 05261. Please indicate that you are responding to the list at the back of this book. Enclose $2.50 for Fourth Class postage or $4.00 for UPS, per order, to cover postage and handling.